Basic Cloud Computing IN 10 DAYS

Basic Cloud Computing IN 10 DAYS

Authored by
Umesh Ganpatrao Dande

WINGS PUBLICATION
WE GIVE WINGS TO YOUR DREAM!

Disclaimer

WINGS PUBLICATION
WE GIVE WINGS TO YOUR DREAM!

Registered Office- 907-Sneh Nagar, Sapna Sangeeta Road,

Agrasen Square, Indore – 452001 (M.P.), India

Website: http://www.wingspublication.com

Email: mybook@wingspublication.com

First Published by WINGS PUBLICATION 2020

Title : Basic Cloud Computing IN 10 DAYS

Price : Rs. 699 I $ 15

ISBN : 978-81-949161-8-5

LIMITS OF LIABILITY/DISCLAIMER OF WARRANTY

Dedicated to my

Handsome Father and Beautiful Mother

Preface

The last day of a database assignment, we had some discussion about cloud computing, which triggered my interest in cloud computing. I was getting amused about cloud capabilities, where you can create VM in a minute, change its dimensions, play with it like playing with a toy. These kinds of things were news for people like us, who have seen, months and months are spent on upgrading the in-house servers. I have seen days where we have to create certain scripts that will kill idle connection on the database server, to get a few MB RAM free for utilization. We use to fight with the development team, asking why they need so much memory for these activities. They use to feel like we are fighting with them for life and death matters. Now it is a cloud, where you can create VM in a minute, with the operating system pre-installed. You have to install the needed software to get your application up and running.

But since it is a public cloud, we had an unavoidable question: How could different client environments install on one cloud? How is security being deployed over here? How can we monitor these resources over the cloud?

We started looking for documentation that will guide us to study cloud computing. Since I always had the internet with me, I started searching for documents over the internet. The more I searched on the internet, the more I got confused. There are a ton and ton of documents and videos over the internet about cloud computing. Some of the videos start with VPC (Virtual Private Cloud), the networking part of cloud computing. When my teammate who worked in development or Quality assurance dept. Will watch this video, in the first couple of hours, they will get fed-up with it. I understand it is the most important part of cloud computing, but very few people understand this networking part in detail.

Certain documentation or video or explaining goes in a monotonous way; they don't have an example or case studies which will explain how to utilize knowedge gained in last min in day to day working. The video will explain things it will not have any mark to stop there; study more about it. Do some exercise/ activities about it.

I have more than 15 years of experience in System administration, and database handling with some studies into networking even was struggling to understand certain things. I have to go through tons and tons of documentation and dozens of videos to understand certain concepts. With all these obstacles, I was able to get certified for the AWS cloud.

After that, cloud computing was the only subject that I discussed with friends and colleagues, where I understand people don't have good material to start studies in cloud computing. Certain people working in development or quality assurance or management and sales need an introductory level of information about this cloud. That will help them to work in their fields in this cloud computing era. Like QA person needs minimum DML knowledge to work as a QA person. That is database knowledge for him/her.This book will be useful to them as well. College students need a book which they can refer it to start their studies in the cloud. So I thought to write this book, which will help all these people in cloud computing studies.

Acknowledgment

The world is a better place, thanks to people who develop leaders and lead others . Those are great people who share their valuable time to mentor leaders around us. I especially thank people who endeavour to grow and help other s grow.

Without the experience and support of my peers and publication team, this book would not exist. While writing this book, my technical editor Meha Gupte has helped me a lot. I had a habit of writing a technical project document. Usually these are drafted for people who are into the same technologies. Still, she has suggested very nice editing, which will help this book refer to anyone, even students. Some of my old friends who reviewed like Prakash Gangavatiker and Vivek Palvia, especially thanks to them.

You come across a lot of people in your life. Some of them have left an impression on your upbringing and career . My father has given me one mantra in childhood, "People like solution man than problem creator, create solutions, and be passionate about what you do". He permitted me to attend drawing class at the age of 11; the class was around 40 km away from my home. I was supposed to be only one child who will use public transport to attend it. With these all adverse condition, he never stopped me, asked me to explore on own.

"You should not compare with anyone else; you should compare with yourself only." That means you should see if you recorded 2 min to walk 1km, you should improve it, don't see what someone else recorded. Break your record, and have competition among you and yourself. This one advice by my sister Dr. Yogeshwari Bhat has changed my life in my early childhood days. My mother always protected me like a small kid; she still thinks we are a little 5-year kid. She has never let us go out of the boundaries of family norms.

There is one name which we can't forget Shree Baliram Gadve sir from Nutan Vidalaye, Umri, and a special thank you. We have troubled you with a lot of non-sense questions about the English language. Ex Principal of Govt Poly Jintur college, Shree V S Deshmukh sir, always given me strength, always available over the phone for any discussion, still has some solution for every problem we are discussing. His rich experience of life and teaching has helped us a lot. Milind Chaple and P S Patil are two people who supported, guided me in my IT journey. I still remember the Oracle Database class we use to take in Aurangabad. Mahesh Ayati is a wonderful HR person, and he had given me strength when I was losing hope in the IT field.

Pravin Bhedurkar, one person I have met in Hyderabad. What was shared between us in Hyderabad is that we both are from Maharashtra. When I shifted to Aurangabad, he forced me to do IBM DB2 certification. He used to call me from Delhi weekly or bi-weekly, use scold on me to finish the studies of db2 and go for certification. I was a Frog in that Aurangabad manufacturing IT world; he asked me to come out of that.

When you live in a housing society, confident people around you have an impression on your life. These people will teach you, guide you in your daily activities. Shree Anuj Jaiswal Manager in IBM, Lokesh Kumar, Sandeep Chaugule, Vikas Jakune, Principle Renuka Singh madam, Prof Dhimant Panchal from MIT School of Design, Ravi Shankar, Pankaj Jha and Special his father Jha uncle, these people have guided me, helped me in good and bad times. Whenever I approached Vikram Shewale for any difficulties, he was always available to listen to it; he is one person who is still positive in all situations. Rahul Shewale is one more person who helped us when we use to work for our housing society.

We use to visit my grandmother's house during summer vacation. She was a rigorous person who use to love us very much. I have seen her make decisions in difficult conditions. She made a tremendous impact on our life. My uncle (mother's brother) Ramesh Pathrikar and Kalidas Pathrikar with these men, I use to get impressed with his neat and clean clothes and the way they use to talk. Jitendra Pathak is one more person who has taught us how to keep your family intact.

My wife has given me strength whenever I feel low in life; she stood the living wall in every situation beside me. I can still remember, when we were buying our home, I was hesitating to buy that house, it was out of my planned budget, but she has said ' Let's buy it, nothing will go wrong. And but still, if something goes wrong, we will relocate to the rented house.' With this kind of word, you get tons of strength with it. My younger brother Avinash and sister Ujjwala has helped me every time we need them.

You meet many people in life, and you learn small things from everyone. Some people name might not be here, but I want to thank you and everyone for helping, guiding me in my good and bad days.

Disclaimer

Certain images referred here are collected from amazon and other blogs are referred here for better understanding of the subject. These are referred here for educational purpose only. Case studies and lab which are discussed in this book are the personal experience of the author. The methods discussed in this book is one of the ways to solve the problem. There might be other methods to solve it; the author doesn't claim that these are the only way to solve it.

Table of Contents

Day 1
3 case studies

CHAPTER One

Introduction to Cloud

CHAPTER POINTS

- **What is Cloud computing?**
- **What are the challenges faced in the in-premises set-up?**
- **How has the cloud helped with this?**
- **What are the advantage and disadvantages of cloud vs. in-premises set-up?**

Computing is the power built by the people for the people. You can create a generic virtual machine with few clicks. The virtual machine can be attached with terabytes of storage. If your application needs more computing power, then it can be added or reduce. This is the beauty of cloud computing. Anyone can create an account on the public cloud and customize the requirements. Cloud computing is available in the form of a free trial version as well.

1.1 History of Cloud Computing

Cloud computing was first seen in Compaq's Intel document in 1996, but it was popularized by Amazon company, releasing its EC2 (Elastic Compute Cloud) product in 2006. The term cloud was actually referred to as the Internet. In the '90s, the Internet has turned desktop-based software into a client and server model. People were amazed by the fact that data used to travel over the wire from one location to another location.

A computer is a machine that can be instructed to carry out sequences of arithmetic or logical operations automatically via computer programming. Modern computers can follow generalized sets of operations, called programs. People started using it as a device that can do the calculation. After that, the concept of LAN (Local Area Network) was in the industry, and with it, the server and client concept was invented. The industry used to have servers such as Mainframe, Novel, or UNIX flavor, and they used to have a client as dump terminals, as shown in the below figure.

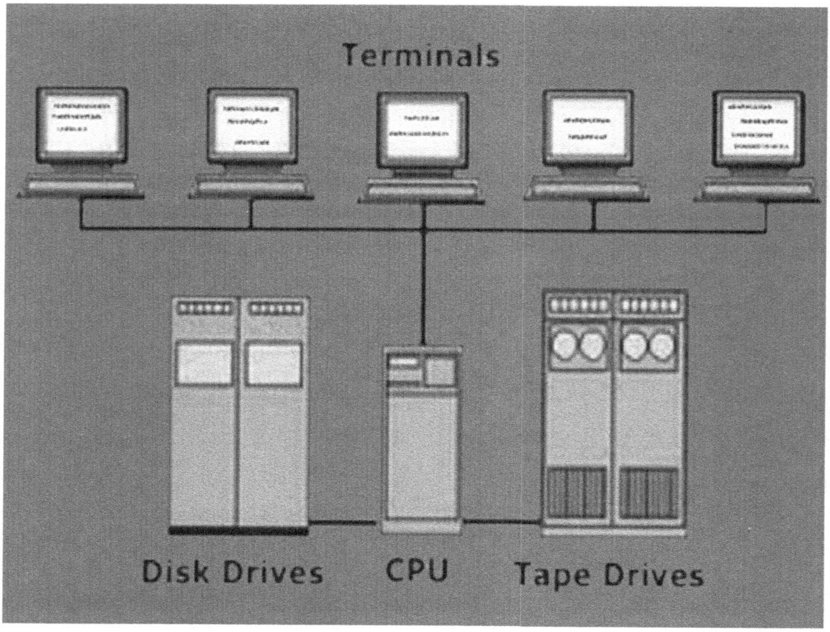

Figure 1

This type of system was utilized in the IT industry for a long time. You need to have a Floppy disk to externalize the data from LAN. Then Windows operating system has taken a very big lead in the industry on a personal computer front. On the server-side, still, the one set of hardware is equal to one server; this was the mechanism. Infrastructure hosting was getting popularised.

One big milestone for cloud computing was the invention of VM (Virtual Machine). In computer science, virtualization is a modern method established in the late 1990s and is unlike simulation and emulation. Virtualization employs techniques used to create instances of an environment, as opposed to simulation, which models the environment, or emulation, which replicates the target environment, such as certain kinds of virtual machine environments.

In the '90s commercial dial-up started to connect to the Internet to transfer the data from one place to another.

In 2000 mid-era the Internet revolution started. A study showed that in 2008 only 10% of adults had a dial-up connection, others were using broadband connections. I had traveled to the USA in August 2009; we had a high-speed broadband connection in our guest house. It was the same time when Amazon had first launched its product EC2.

At that time, companies were offering a dedicated server for rent. Rackspace, Satyam Infoway, was some companies from the USA and India that used to offer dedicated servers. These servers were situated at the company's data center, and customers accessed them over the Internet. Hosting companies were providing the server with an operating system installed on it. Customers needed to install the database and its application.

We had used the Rackspace server to install some of an application for famous retail in the USA like Barnes and Noble (B & N), Toys R Us, and so on. However, this company, where I used to work, has started the software as a Service (SaaS) model in back 2008. At that time, Rackspace was offering Infrastructure as a Service (IaaS) to provide a dedicated server / VM. The term IaaS was rarely used, but it was considered as the hosted server. Applications had server and client architecture. In the early 2000s Flash or Java applets were used for client-server architect applications.

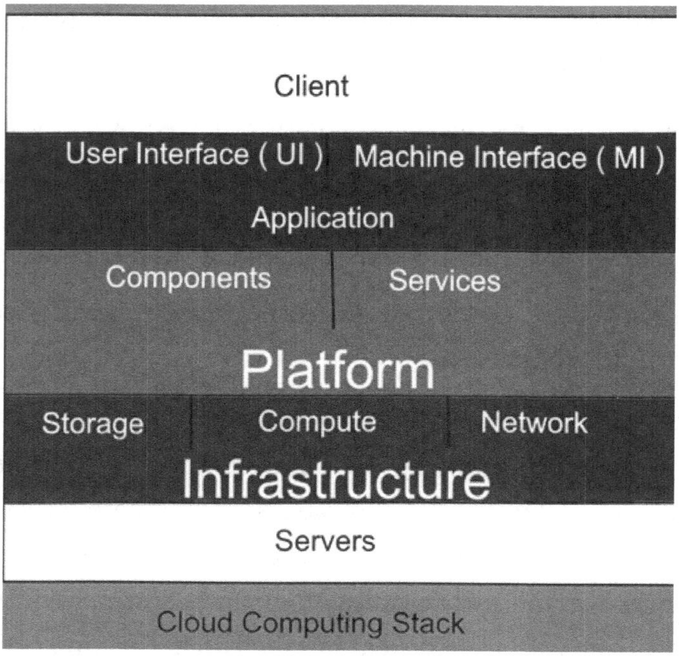

Figure 2

1.2 Limitations of on-site Hardware Set-up

There are many articles, videos, and tutorials on the Internet that are talking about the cloud. But someone may ask, "when you can have servers in your data center, on-site. You can connect these servers to the Internet so as it can serve its service to worldwide users. Then why the cloud is needed? And now, Why we need a cloud?" What problems can be addressed by using cloud computing? We will try to understand these factors in this section of the book. We will see/discuss certain infrastructure cases where the in-premises set-up has limitations. Let us elaborate on cloud computing and how it will be useful in day-to-day activities.

Case Study:1

Context

A customer had the online product website with the set-up as shown in the below figure. It has an application server cluster, three servers participating in it. Using a classic load balancer, requests are sent to the cluster. It has a two-database server, the first active, and another one for DR purposes.

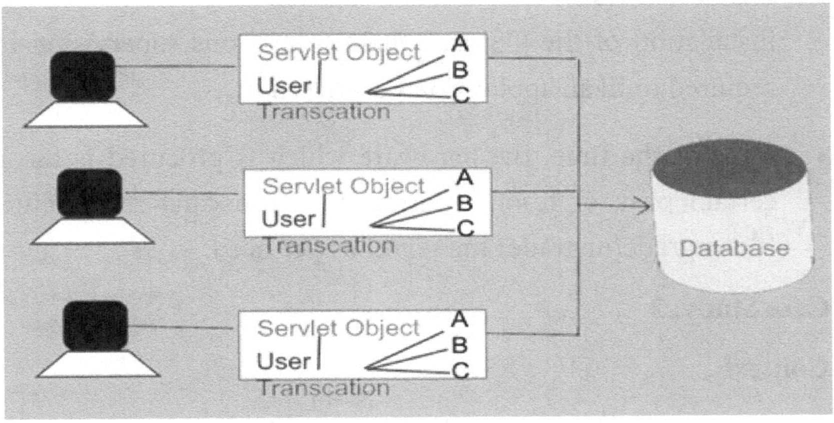

Figure 3

Challenge

Over time as the user base gets an increase, then we must need to upgrade hardware to perform streamlined operations. It takes a lot of time to get the correct level of the latest compatible hardware. Once the management approves the purchase of the hardware, the company process takes a lot of time to place an order of the same. After all these issues, when hardware reaches the company premises, it again takes a lot of time to get assembled, needs to plan downtime, interacts with the concerned team for downtime. Provided hardware is in good condition/configuration; still, it takes a couple of days to install the operating system, middleware, and database.

Outcome

- It has a capital expenditure process.
- Once the management approves the hardware, it takes a few months to receive the correct hardware.
- The system admin does not have the facility to check/test the configuration before procurement.
- Additional resources are required, such as experts, to do the installation of the OS, and their continuous supervision is required until an application becomes live.
- Most of the time, the hardware which is procured is for a certain peak of resource utilization. You can't reconfigure (downgrade/upgrade) the server as per need.

Case Study: 2

Context

A customer had an online employee Human Resource website with the set-up, as shown in the below figure. It has a six-application server to create a cluster. By using this cluster load balancer, requests are distributed among an application server. Since this is an HR kind of application, it has maximum traffic at every last and first week of the month. For the rest of all month, the server was not being utilized to 30% of their resource.

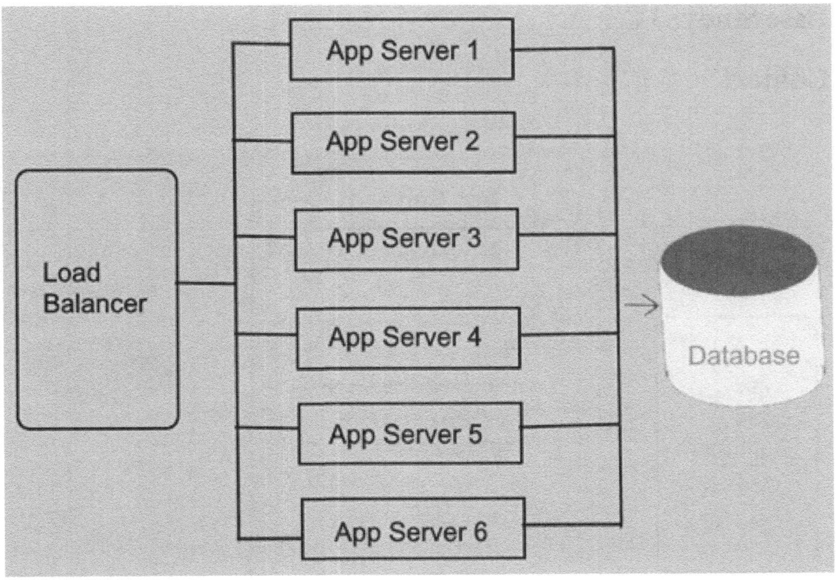

Figure 4

Challenge

As we can see, the resource is under-utilized most of the time. Since it's an HR Application traffic is heavy on first and last weeks of the month, hence server utilization is less than 30% for the remaining weeks.

Outcome

- The system receives load at only two weeks of the month. Thus, the system is in-utilized for at least 75 % time.
- In this situation, for the rest of the days, the system admin cannot take the resource away from the cluster, as it requires many processes of installation.

Case Study: 3

Context

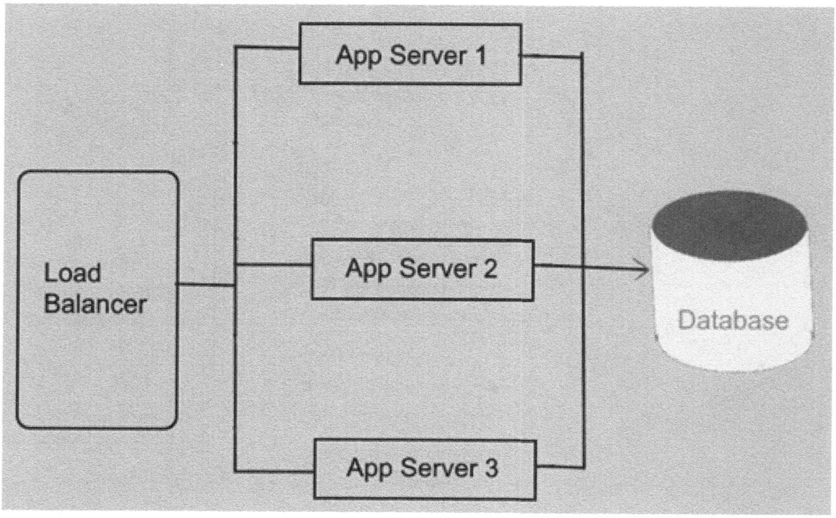

Figure 5

A customer had a development shop, and their products were available in the market. They were providing customized solutions to the application for their clients. The major part of the application was the same, but for a specific client, a minor part of it-enhanced.

Challenge

One of the clients was facing an issue with the enhanced code. The client was using open-source resources to run that application. We asked them to share their database (as it was not large). As the client had a development shop, they already had the necessary resources to do such type of application testing. The system admin team needs to set- up such an environment to test the application and database. The application with an enhanced part was rebuild.

1.3 Why we need Cloud?

The above three case studies have shown us the limitations of the in-premises Data Center/hardware. How can the cloud be useful in these cases? Let us discuss it further.

The Solution of Case Study: 1

The application was hosted on a dedicated server. So it needed a lot of time to upgrade. Whereas depending upon the type of cloud, i.e., IaaS, PaaS, or SaaS (Just keep these terms in mind, for now, we will discuss it further in detail) can help you to upgrade the configuration of the server in few minutes. In this way, the efforts of the system admin can reduce.

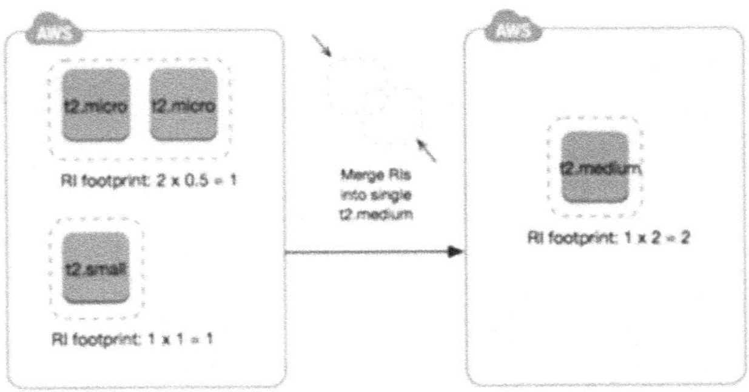

Figure 6

Your infrastructures can built-in a couple of hours; you can test the application by using the same infrastructure. Moreover, on the requirement, you can make changes to server resources or choose another image. The Interesting part is that no CapEx investment is required for such type of set-up. This means that you have to pay as per your use. The Server image (VM, IAM) already has an operating system installed on it. You can have some boot script, which can install the required software like application servers such as IIS or Apache and so on.

The Solution of Case Study: 2

This specific application is regarding the company employee portal or some similar type of application. This type of application can have a pick load for a specific time. Compute resources get ideal for 75% time of an application.

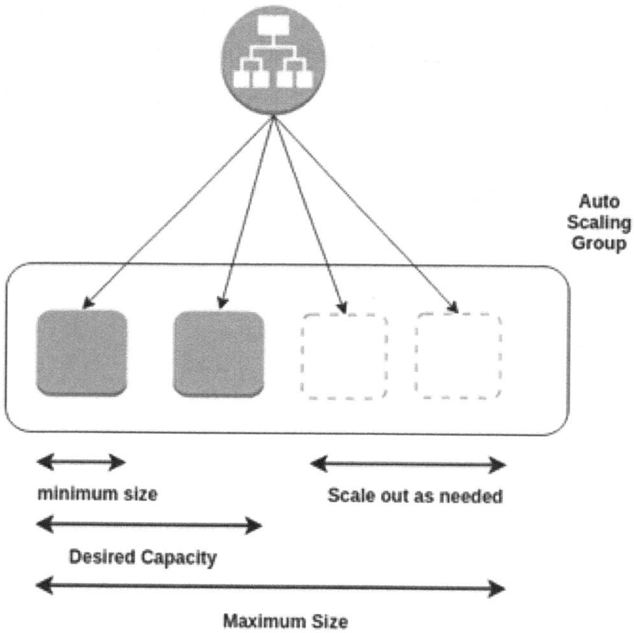

Figure 7

With cloud computing, an application can work with a minimum scale of resources, even in ideal conditions. Whenever it requires more computing resources, it can be added to the requirement. With such type of system, it can serve to peak computing level of application.

Automatically it will decommission extra-added compute resources when the system is having very little load on the application. Using this, it can save the excess allocated compute power.

The Solution of Case Study: 3

This specific type of case can be noticed in almost every development center. In this case, you need to make a similar set-up that is present at the client location for the reproduction of the same error. Companies need to have dedicated hardware planned for such type of situation. The bottom line is, this type of situation may happen a couple of times in a year, which can make this compute resource set ideal when there is no requirement.

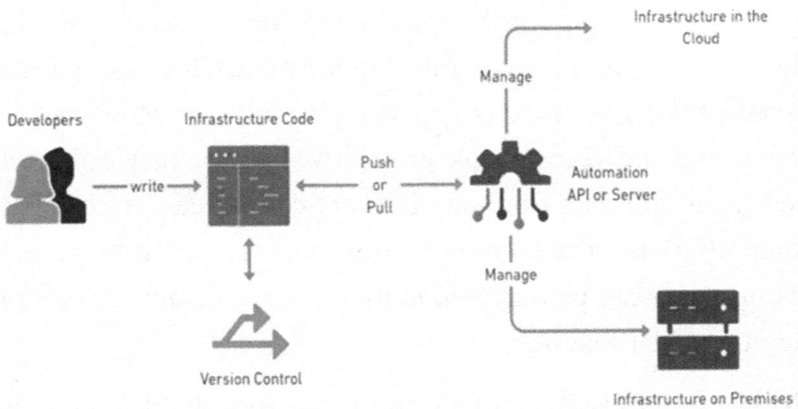

Figure 8

Cloud has helped this organization, with one of the features of cloud computing called infrastructure as code (IaC). With this feature of the cloud, the user can create the infrastructure in a couple of minutes. You can write the script, which will help to set up VPC (network part), EC2 instance (VM/Server), and all other facilities like the file system or VPC gateway.

You can use this set-up (Infrastructure) until the root cause of the problem is noticed. After that, you can remove it. One of the set-ups where this script was scheduled/automated to make this setup up and running till day start and its use to erase the set up at night time.

The above examples clearly explain how the cloud can be useful to overcome the limitations of in-premises issues.

1.4 How Businesses use Cloud Computing

You are probably using cloud computing at work, too. Just like your personal email, your business email may also be cloud-based. Other business uses of the cloud include- collaboration and communication, productivity, file backup, data analysis, tools for developing software, and more. Many organizations use cloud-based apps through a subscription model. It is cost-effective because the organization only pays for what it uses. Moreover, it is convenient and keeps people productive because they can access their apps and data from any Internet-connected device. Cloud computing also makes many business processes more reliable because data can be mirrored at multiple redundant sites on the cloud provider's network.

Here are some examples of how businesses use cloud computing:

Communication

The cloud gives users easy, web-based access to communication and collaboration tools like email and calendaring. Messaging, voice, and video calling apps like Skype can also take advantage of the cloud. Your messages and information are located on the service provider's network rather than on your personal device.

Productivity

Office tools (like Microsoft Office 365) can be cloud-based, allowing you to connect to your most-used apps over the Internet. You can work on your document, presentation, or spreadsheet software from anywhere. As your information stored in the cloud, you do not have to worry about losing your data if in case your device fails. Many apps can run directly from your web browser without any need to download or install special software.

Business Processes

Many sophisticated business applications such as customer relationship management, enterprise resource planning, and document management can be rented from the cloud service provider. This ensures the availability and security of your organization's business-critical resources and lets you access these tools conveniently through the web browser.

File Storage

The cloud can be used for file storage. The advantage for you is an easy backup. Many cloud services automatically synchronize your files from your desktop. Also, if you switch to a different computer or mobile device, you can still retrieve your files. Organizations pay only for the used storage. They do not have to maintain the infrastructure. The cloud service provider maintains it.

Backup and Recovery

When your organization relies on cloud services for backup and recovery, it can avoid capital outlay for infrastructure and management. The cloud service provider is responsible for managing data and meeting legal and compliance requirements. The cloud also provides higher flexibility in that it can accommodate unpredictable storage and backup demands. Your cloud service provider can also make fast recovery because your organization's assets are located over a network of physical locations rather than at one on-site data center.

Application Development

The cloud can help you to create quick cross-platform experiences in web development, mobile apps, and gaming apps. This can scale up business as the user base grows. Many cloud services include pre-coded tools such as directory services, search, and security that can give speed to your development and simplify it.

Test and Development

The cloud can provide an environment to help you to save costs and bring your apps quickly to the market. You do not need to secure budgets and spend valuable project time and resources to set-up the physical environments. Your team can quickly set-up and disassemble test and development environments in the cloud. You can scale these dev-test environments up or down depending upon your needs.

Big Data Analytics

Cloud computing can help your organization to do data analyses. The data can be analyzed by its patterns and insights. You can make predictions, improve forecasting, and make other business decisions. Cloud services can provide high processing power and sophisticated tools for mining a massive amount of data. Moreover, it also possesses the ability to scale your environment quickly as your data grows.

1.5 History of AWS in Cloud Computing

- 2002- AWS services launched
- 2006- Launched its cloud products
- 2012- Holds first customer event
- 2015- Reveals revenues achieved of $4.6 billion

- 2016- Surpassed $10 billion revenue target
- 2016- Release snowball and snowmobile
- 2019- Offers nearly 100 cloud services

1.6 Advantages and Disadvantages of Cloud Computing

The following are the advantage and disadvantages of cloud computing.

Sr. No.	Advantage of cloud	Disadvantages of cloud
1	Cost Saving	Security Threat in cloud
2	High Speed	Downtime
3	Backup and restore of data	Technical Issues
4	Auto software integration	Lack of support
5	Unlimited storage capacity	Performance can vary
6	Quick Deployment	Internet Connectivity

Advantage

- Cost-saving: Most interesting thing about cloud computing is services are free from capital expenses. There are no huge costs of the hardware in cloud computing. You just have to pay as you operate it and enjoy the model based on your subscription plan.

Lets move forward to second day, where we will discuss regarding types of cloud.

♦ ♦

Day 2
type of clouds

CHAPTER *Two*

Type of Clouds and Differences

CHAPTER POINTS

- **How many types of cloud are there?**
- **What is the difference between these clouds?**
- **Which kind of cloud is used at what time?**
- **What is the procedure for the AWS trial account?**

Cloud computing is Internet-based in which a shared pool of computing resources is available over the network. It can rapidly operate and released with minimal management without any interaction with the service provider. Based on the position of the cloud concerning a group of people (organization) or individual accessing it via the Internet, it can differentiate in the following way:

1. Public Cloud
2. Private Cloud
3. Hybrid Cloud
4. Community Cloud

Public Cloud: AWS has a major share across the cloud computing industry. It is managed by a third- party, which provides cloud services over the Internet to the public. This type of cloud service provider offers solutions to minimizing IT infrastructure costs. It offers good options for small or start-up companies to start their operation by investing in hardware and other services. Moreover, it offers services, which include front end and backend database services. The fundamental characteristic of the public cloud is multitenancy. It serves multiple users with an isolated infrastructure of their own. It has other facilities such as pay as you use. It generally has its resources on provider's data centers that may be located across the globe.

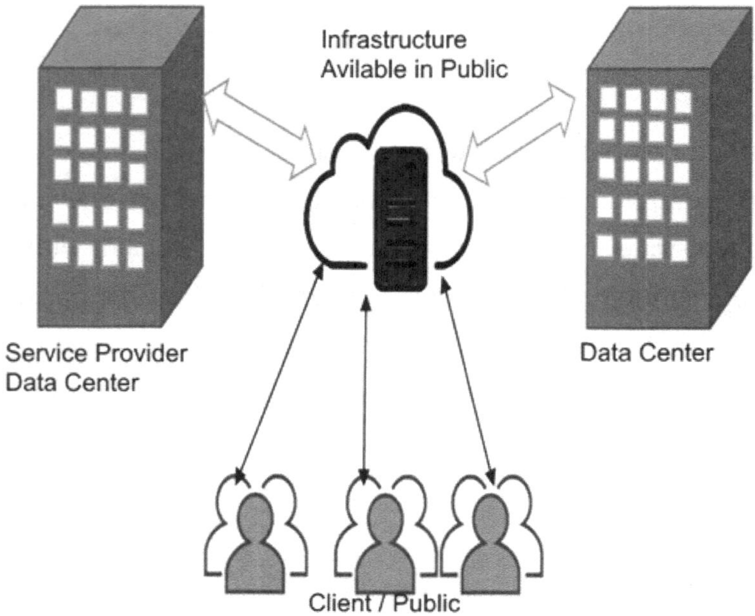

Figure 9

AWS is one of the famous public clouds which is available to use. AWS offers 12-month free usage as well.

Follow the instructions to open a free trial account on AWS.

1. Go to **https://aws.amazon.com/.**

2. Click **Create an AWS Account.** An AWS account creates window displays.

Figure 10

Important	Make sure that you are providing the correct information. Otherwise, you will not be able to access your account.

Note

- If "Create a new AWS account" is not visible, then first select Sign in to a different account and then click Create a new AWS account.
- If you have logged in to AWS in recent times, it may say Sign in to the console.

3. Enter the required details and click **Continue.**

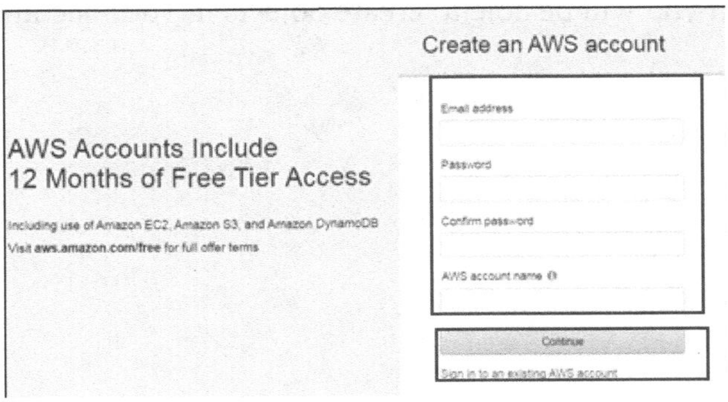

Figure 11

4. You will receive an email from AWS.

Important	• Since the information you provided is correct, you will get an email with further instructions. Else you will not be able to access your account. • If "Create a new AWS account" is not visible, then first select Sign in to a different account, and then select Create a new AWS account.

5. Select the optional button, **Personal** or **Professional**.

Note Personal and professional, both accounts have the same features and functions.

6. Enter the required details.

Note Make sure that you have read and understood the terms of AWS.

7. Clear the checkbox of terms of the AISPL Customer Agreement and then click **Create Account and Continue.**

Once an account is created, you will receive an email from amazon. To activate your created account you need to verify it by giving your credit/debit card details. Once the verification is done only then you will be able to create objects in your account.

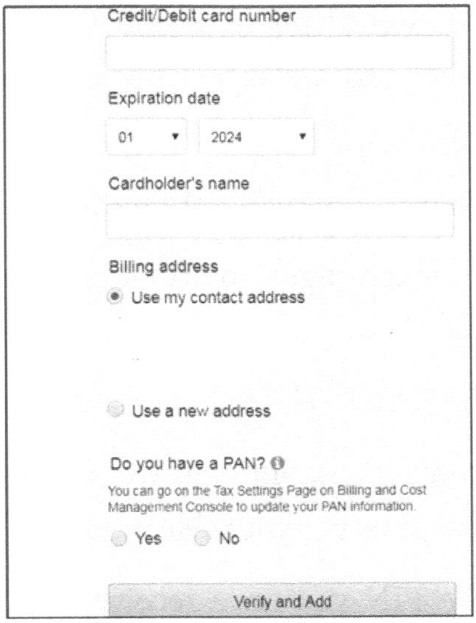

Figure 12

Following is the procedure to add the payment method.

1. On the Payment Information page, select **Payment methods.**

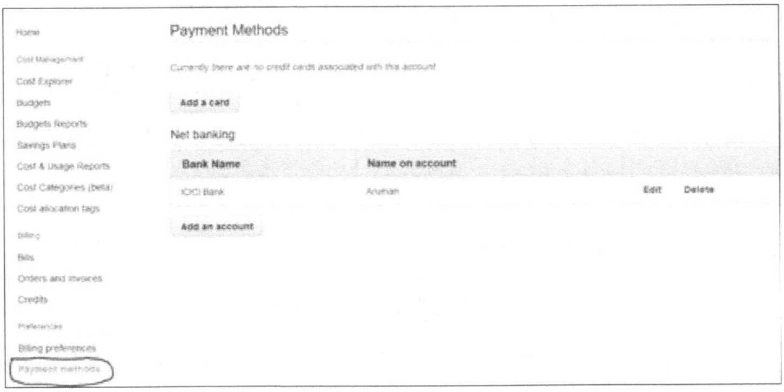

Figure 13

Note

- Payment information is secure, and it is necessary to verify your identity through it. AWS is free to use up to the free tier limits.
- Rs 2 (for India) is deducted from the given payment information account.

Amazon also verifies your phone number. Verification is done either by voice call or text message. Choose the way you want to verify your account.

1. Select your country code from the drop-down.
2. Enter your ten digits smartphone number, which you want to get validated.
3. Enter the CAPTCHA to confirm that you are a human
4. Select contact me, and you will receive a voice call or text message as per your selection.
5. Enter the PIN you have received by text message or voice call and click **Continue**.
6. Choose the AWS support plan you requiring in this account.

The customers get basic support, which includes:

- **Customer Service & Communities** - 24x7 access to customer service, documentation, whitepapers, and support forums.
- **AWS Trusted Advisor** - Access to the seven core trusted advisor checks and guidance to provision your resources by following best practices to increase performance and improve security.
- **AWS Personal Health Dashboard** - A personalized view of the health of AWS services and alerts when your resources are impacted.

Note This support section will have at least one or two questions in the certification exam

Topic	Developer	Business	Enterprise
AWS Trust Advisor Best practice check.	Seven core checks.	Full set check.	Full set check.
Enhanced Technical Support.	Email access to cloud support associates during business hours. It will have one contact per account.	24x7 phone, email, and chat with a support engineer. Unlimited case.	24x7 phone, email, and chat with a support engineer. Unlimited case.
Response time	General guidance in less than 24 business hours. Less than 12 business hours, support for a broken system.	To the addition of dev support 1. Support in Less than 4 hours for production system not work. 2. Production server down will be attended in less than an hour.	It will have a business type of support. In addition to it, you will get support in less than 15 minutes for a critical business system.

Topic	Developer	Business	Enterprise
Architect Guideline	General	Context to your use case	The support engineer will study your application, and it will provide the consultative type of support.
Third-Party Software Support	-	Interoper-ability and Configuration Guidelines	Interoperability and Configuration Guidelines.
Technical Support	-	-	Designated Technical Account Manager (TAM).
Training	-	-	Access to online self-paced labs.

Note Your account may take the time up to 24 hours to activate.

Once you receive the confirmation email from Amazon about your account activation, you can start working on it. You will have your free tier account setup. You can create/use an object which is enabled in the free tier.

Private Cloud: This is a computing resource that is hosted for a specific organization. It gives the user a facility to the dynamic provision to create resources. It is more of a dedicated environment that delivers a similar advantage to the public cloud, including scalability, improved resource utilization, and self-service capabilities while retaining isolation.

It provides user secured shell. It enhances the security of dedicated servers, physically isolated network, and compute and storage layer.

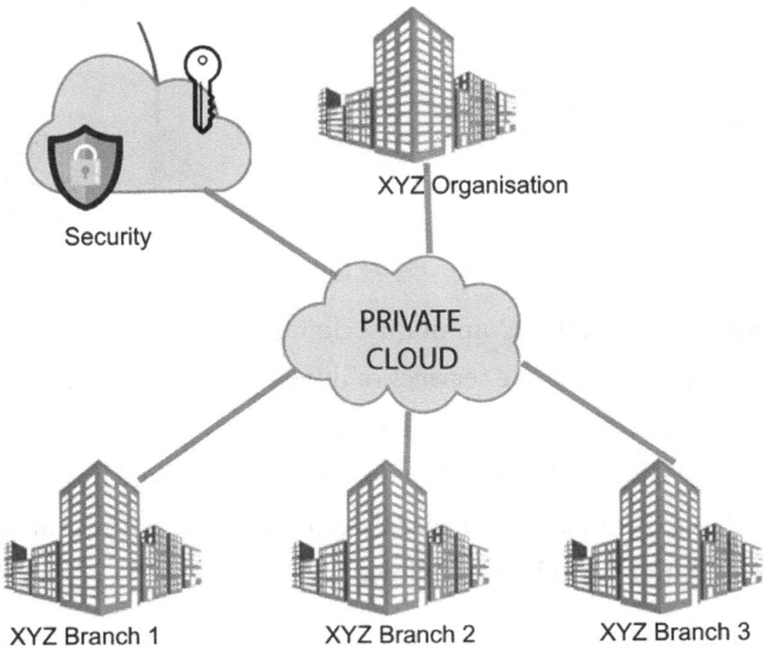

Figure 14

Hybrid Cloud: This is a heterogeneous distributed setup that resulted in clubbing the features and facilities of both public and private cloud. It is also known as a heterogeneous cloud because of its heterogeneous set. It works as a solution to overcome the limitations of both public and private clouds. The private cloud has a drawback to scale-up on demand. It faces issues to address peak loads. So, to overcome these difficulties, we need a hybrid cloud.

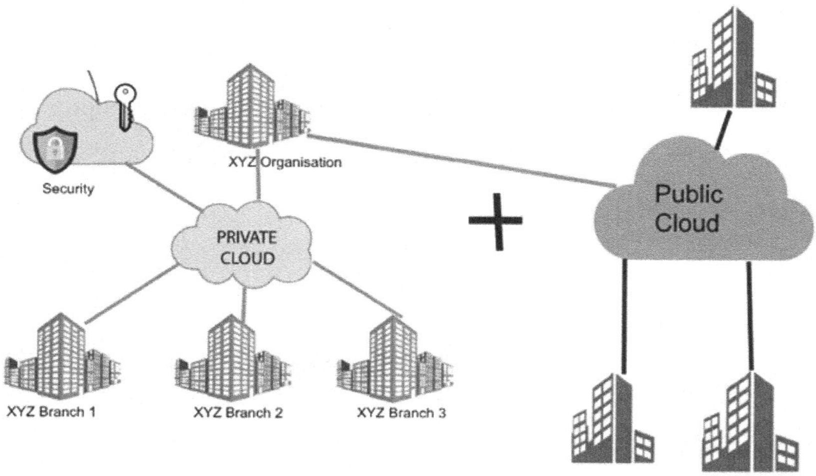

Figure 15

Community Cloud: Community clouds are distributed systems created by clubbing the services of different clouds to address the specific need of a specific business sector, community, or industry. These type of cloud system have shared infrastructure by business who has a common task or shared concern. Some of the examples of community cloud are as following:

- **Media Industry:** It has a community cloud where they have low cost, quick, and simple content generation medium.

- **Healthcare Industry:** It uses such type of infrastructure to share the formation of knowledge on a global level.
- **Academic Publishing:** The research papers are published by researchers across the globe.

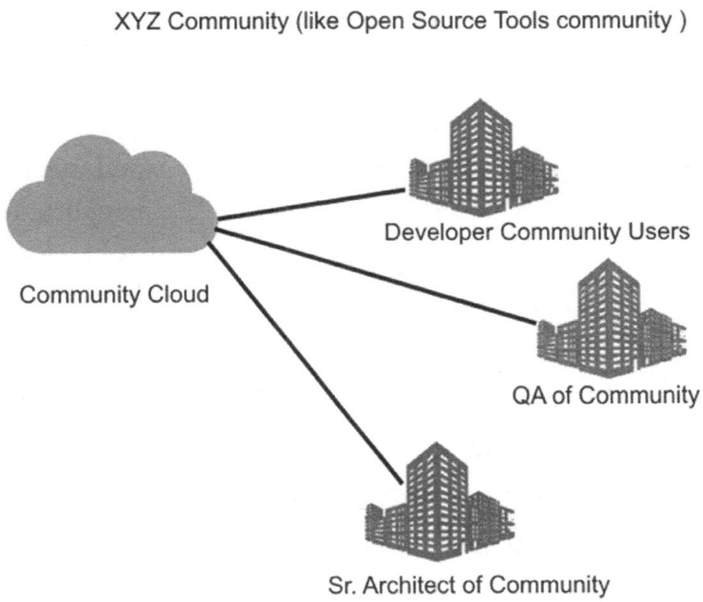

Figure 16

The following are the differences between these clouds:

Topic	Private Cloud	Public Cloud	Hybrid Cloud
Infrastructure	Single-Tenant: It has dedicated hardware and a network it can be managed by a highly skilled support team.	Multi-Tenant: Cost is low because many other companies are securely using the same platforms. All resources are managed by the service provider.	It is higher than the public but lower than Private.

Topic	Private Cloud	Public Cloud	Hybrid Cloud
Business Requirement	High security, performance, and customization with control options.	It can be selected if you are looking for pay as you grow a type of facility. Usually, it is selected for affordable solutions.	It can be selected if you need some sort of in-house security to be applied with the resource in a public cloud, such as an application that has Active Directory Authentication.
Best Use	When you have more sensitive user data or financial data.	It is mainly used for public-facing applications and capacity testing purpose	This type of set-up can be used for QA/ test purposes.
Scalability	More resources are required to enhance scalability.	Very easy to scale it. With a certain click of buttons, it can be scaled to its double capacity.	This has a public cloud that can be easily scaled.

Topic	Private Cloud	Public Cloud	Hybrid Cloud
Support and Maintenance	An in-house, highly skilled technical team is required.	Cloud service providers do support it with economic costing.	It needs technical resources with economic support from the cloud provider.
Cost	It is a costlier one among these clouds. It needs upfront a high cost for hardware implementation, software licensing, and skilled technical staff to implement the same. It is the CapEx type of model.	This has the facility to pay as you grow. You can control costs in many ways. It is OpEx driven model.	It is a combination of both.

Based on cloud services, the cloud can be differentiated in the following way:

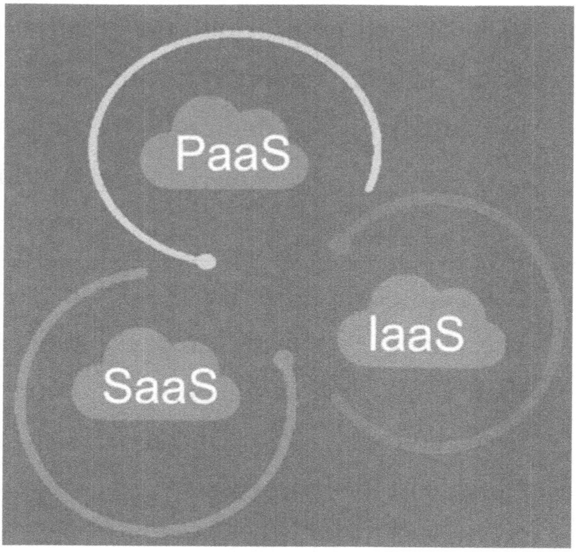

Figure 17

1. IaaS
2. SaaS
3. PaaS

Let us discuss these cloud services further:

IaaS (Infrastructure as a Service): The name itself suggests that the vendor for such type of services provides the infrastructure to host the operating system and application on these servers. IaaS allows businesses to allocate resources/compute power as required. Customers don't need to look for the hardware of the same. It will create a virtual machine with the required configuration. It also delivers computing infrastructure such as network, storage, and operating system through virtualization.

These services are typically provided through the dashboard

or an API. It provides complete control to the client's overall infrastructure build for it. IaaS provides the same capabilities as traditional data centers, whereas it is managed by the service provider. You can directly access all these resources which are there in the virtual data center.

IaaS characteristics can be listed in the following way:

- All resources such as Virtual Server, Network, and File System are available as a service.
- The vendor of these services charges per minute or on an hourly basis. So, it affects cost as you use these resources.
- These resources are highly scalable. You can add storage or RAM to the server within a fraction of minutes.
- Multiple users are allowed to work on the same resources.
- Organizations retain full control over it, though these servers are virtual.
- These resources are very dynamic and flexible to use. Like if you have created a Virtual Private Network (VPC), servers added to it will get updated automatically in the subnet defined over here.

IaaS is typically used by many startup companies that don't want to purchase a large set of hardware. It is used by an application that required a dynamic changing capacity. Large companies need full control over their resources, which is provided by IaaS. If you are not sure about the application demand for resources, IaaS is a good choice.

Examples of IaaS can be AWS of Amazon, Azure by Microsoft, GCE by Google and Digital Ocean, and so on.

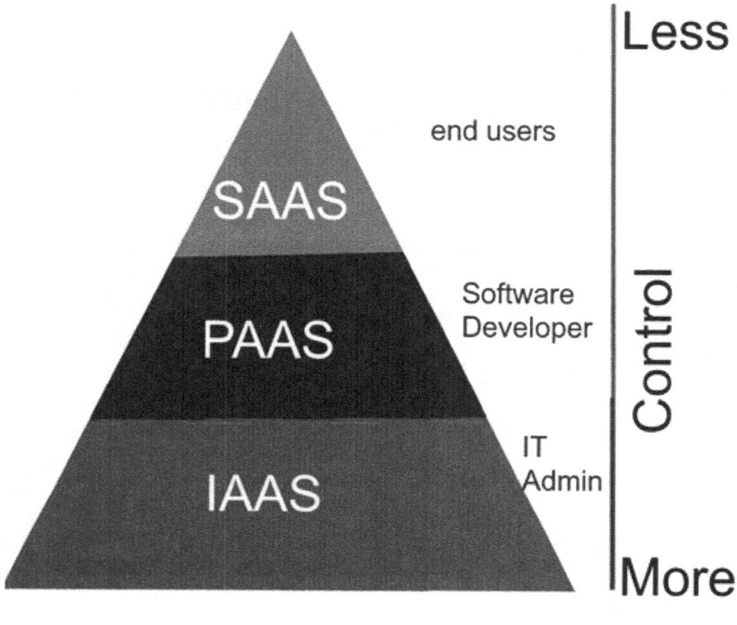

Figure 18

PaaS (Platform as a Service): It is used as a platform to host certain types of applications, such as Google App Engine. It provides a framework for developers to built their applications and user services to customize the same. In this specific cloud, the service provider takes care of the entire infrastructure. At the same time, developers are supposed to manage their applications.

It is quite similar to the SaaS model where software is delivered to the end-user, where the developer has given to build an application using the framework put across by the service provider as it is being delivered to the developer by using the web interface, so as developers do not have to worry about the operating system, software updates, or storage, which is managed by the service provider.

PaaS characteristic can be listed in the following way:

- It is more simple and cost-effective for the development and deployment of apps.
- It is a highly stable platform.
- It can be more trusted as it is highly available.
- It helps the developer to focus on the customization of the app rather than the working of the software.
- It is easy to migrate to a hybrid model.

PaaS is specifically helpful for companies that have extensive work on app development. The developers can start working on the customization of the application with minimal cost. This platform can be easily integrated with other vendor development work.

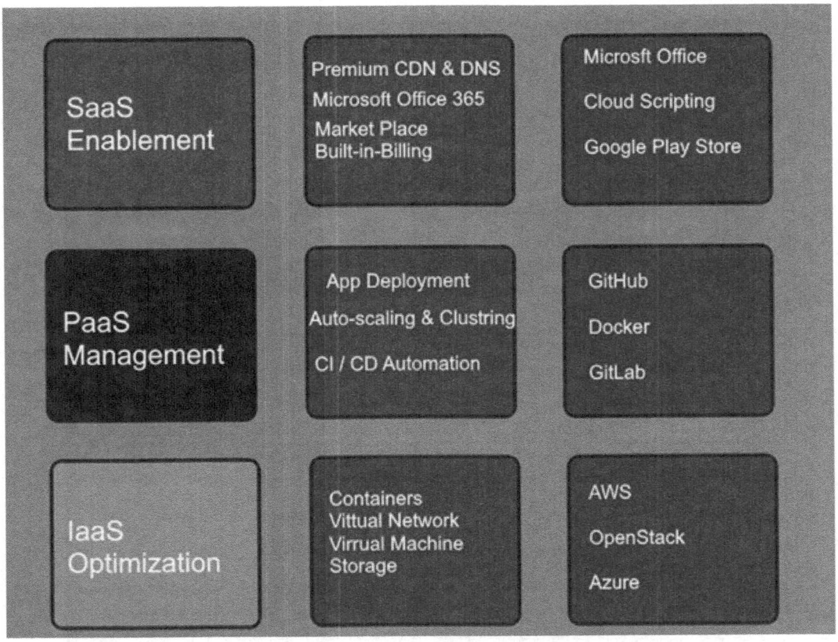

Figure 19

SaaS (Software as a Service): It is commonly known as cloud application services, mostly used to deliver applications. It is a platform where applications are hosted to service provider infrastructure, and customers can directly access it from there. A majority of applications run through a web browser only, which means you do not need to download or install any application on your device.

One more common application for this type of cloud can be seen as the marketplace. Google play store is a big application that can be seen as a SaaS platform. As it has a web delivery model, it eliminates the requirement to download it to any individual computer. SaaS vendor manages all middleware applications, databases, and storage resulting in a well-maintained platform.

SaaS characteristic can be listed in the following way:

- This platform is centrally managed by the SaaS vendor.
- As the application is hosted on a remote server, customers do not have access to its infrastructure.
- The user is not responsible for any software or hardware update.

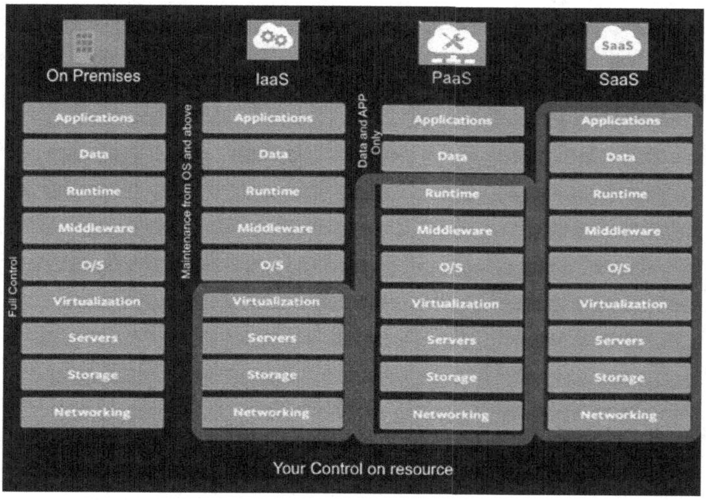

Figure 20

The following are the differences between these clouds:

Topic	IaaS	PaaS	SaaS
Infrastructure	You can create the Virtual Machine, network, and storage required for your application.	You can customize your code. No infrastructure will be offered.	No code customization will be offered. Your application will be hosted to use.
Cost	Pay as you use the number of resources for building your infrastructure.	Pay for the number of applications that are hosted for customizing code.	It might have no. of a user or as per the bandwidth. They were used by the application.
Maintenance	The service provider will provide hardware. The operating system and application maintenance are the client's responsibility.	It is the code you have to maintain. The service provider will take care of the rest of the things.	The service provider will take care of everything.
Scalability	This type of cloud is highly scalable. In this, you can have multiple instances of the server installation. Moreover, here you can have multiple databases or different created networks.	You don't have any visibility on the hardware.	You don't have any visibility on the hardware.

Topic	IaaS	PaaS	SaaS
Technical Staff	Staff is required to maintain this part of the infrastructure.	It is used by the developer team	Staff is not required to maintain it. Everything is taken care of by the service provider
Flexibility	It is more flexible. The same resource can be utilized for many applications.	You are required to purchase another workspace for another development of the application.	No flexibility. You are required to purchase a different plan for the second application.
Usage (Examples)	AWS EC2, Rackspace, DigitalOcean, Magento Enterprise Edition, Google Compute Engine (GCE).	AWS Elastic Beanstalk, Heroku, Force.com, Windows Azure (mostly used as PaaS), OpenShift, Apache Stratos, Magento Commerce Cloud.	Google Apps, Salesforce, Dropbox, Mailchimp, Zendesk, DocuSign, Slack, HubSpot.

Lets end this day over here, next day we will discuss about important aspect of AWS cloud, EC2 instance

♦ ♦

Day 3
Lab - 1
Lab -2

CHAPTER *Three*

EC2 Instance

CHAPTER POINTS

- **What are the different resources available in the cloud?**
- **Does the Image have an operating system installed in it?**
- **Types of EC2 instances available in AWS Cloud?**
- **EC2 gets a static IP address, then why Elastic IP is different from it?**
- **Is it easy to connect to the EC2 server?**
- **Can we use putty for connecting to the EC2 instance?**
- **How can we build an entire application in the cloud using different resources?**

3.1 Introduction to EC2 Instance

EC2 instance in AWS is a virtual machine/server, with predefined hardware configuration and an operating system. In computing, a virtual machine is an image of the system or emulation of the system. A system virtual machine is created by using a hypervisor, which utilizes part of the resources from actually available hardware. Using this technology, we can create multiple instances that can use underline hardware to execute as servers, yet they will be isolated from each other. The modern hypervisor will utilize hardware-assisted virtualization.

Figure 21

EC2 is a virtual server, which will be available with an operating system installed on it. EC2 eliminates CapEx investment for hosting an application or hardware, as it can be rented on a monthly charge basis, required for the development of an application. Here, you can launch as many servers as you are required with network and storage. Amazon has a feature with which you can scale-up, and scale-down the required EC2 instance compute power.

Presently, Amazon EC2 supports the following operating system. You will see a ready image with an operating system installed on it.

- Red Hat Linux
- Ubuntu
- Windows Server
- SUSE Linux Enterprise Server
- Fedora
- Debian
- CentOS
- Gentoo Linux
- Oracle Linux
- FreeBSD
- Amazon Linux

3.2 Instance Types

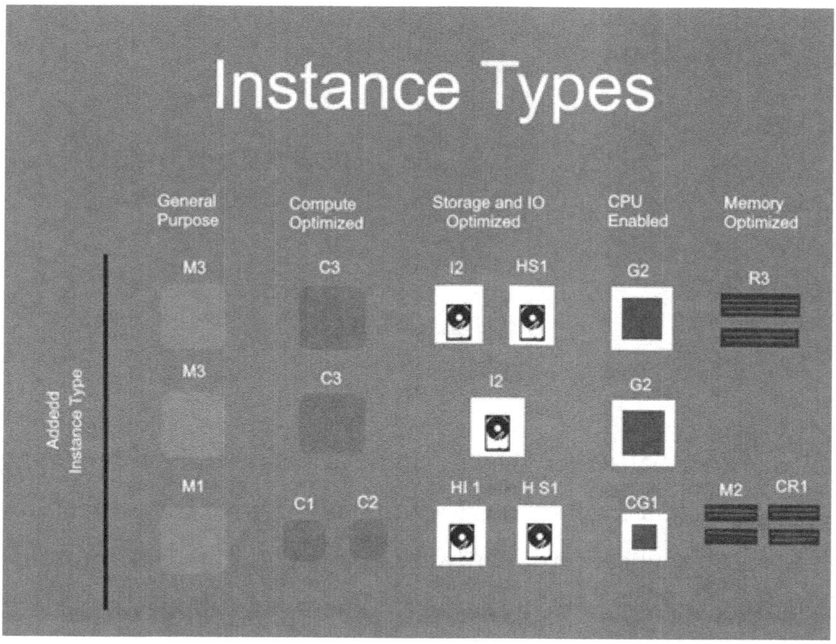

Figure 22

Let's see how the nomenclature is decided for this type of instance.

Type Of Instance	Purpose of Setup	Short Forms			Examples
General Purpose	General-purpose instances provide a balance of computing, memory, and networking resources and can be used for a variety of workloads.	A1	M5 M5a M5d	T2 T3 T3a	• Web Servers • Containerized Microservices • Distributed Data Stores • Backend Server for SAP • Microsoft Share Point
Compute Optimized, the instance with high CPU	These servers formed for the application which required high compute for performance	C1	C4	C5	• Batch Processing Workload • Media Transcoding • Scientific Modeling • Gaming Server
Storage and I/O optimized	These type of servers are designed for the applications which required high I/O read and write	D2	H1	I3	• Data Warehouse's MPP • MapReduce • Log of Data Processing • RDBMS and NoSQL
GPU Enabled	Graphic processing unit enabled machines are used for machine learning	P2	P3	G3	• For Machine Learning • Deep Data Analysis
Memory-Optimized	These types of servers are formed for a memory-intensive application like a database	R4 R5	X1	Z1	• RDBMS and NoSQL Database • Web-Scale Cache Stores • Bigdata Applications

Lab 1-Procedure to Launch an EC2 Instance

Amazon offers many pre-defined instances. Let us see how to launch an EC2 instance for computing purposes. Following are the step by step procedure discussed to launch an EC2 instance.

1. Log in to the **AWS portal**.
2. On the top left corner, click **AWS Services**.

You will find a list of AWS services here. They are broadly categorized like compute, storage, and database, such as if you want to create an EC2 instance, you need to go to a submenu of computing.

3. On the Compute category, select **EC2.**

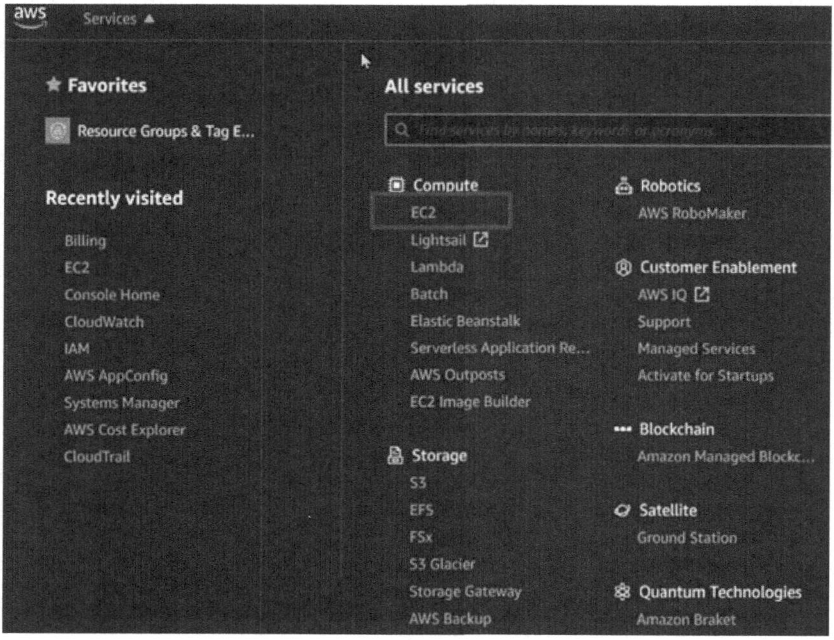

Figure 23

The following dashboard of EC2 is displayed on the screen

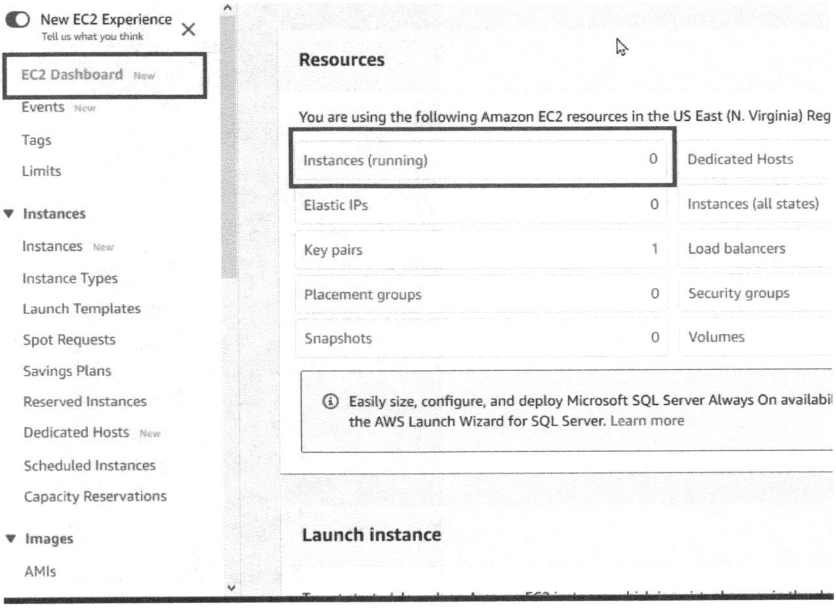

Figure 24

Note This is a new account. So, here no instance is created. By default, it is using a VPC (Networking details will be discussed in the next session).

4. On the top right corner, you can see a list of Regain and Availability zones. Select the **AZ**[1] of your choice to create the EC2 instance.

[1]Availability zone is called as AZ's; it is bunch of data centre cluster as one AZ.

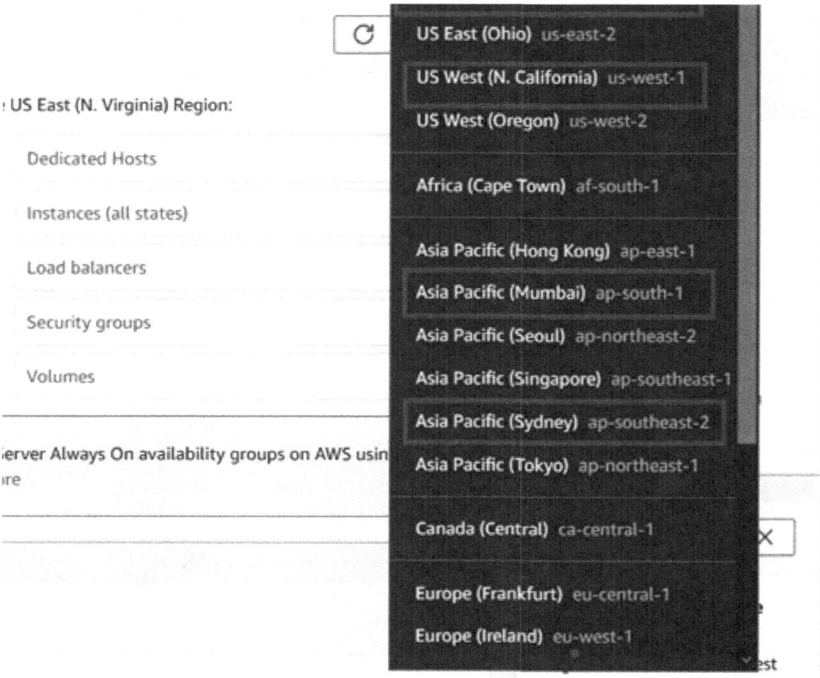

Figure 25

Once you have selected the regain and availability zone, you can see the launch instance button.

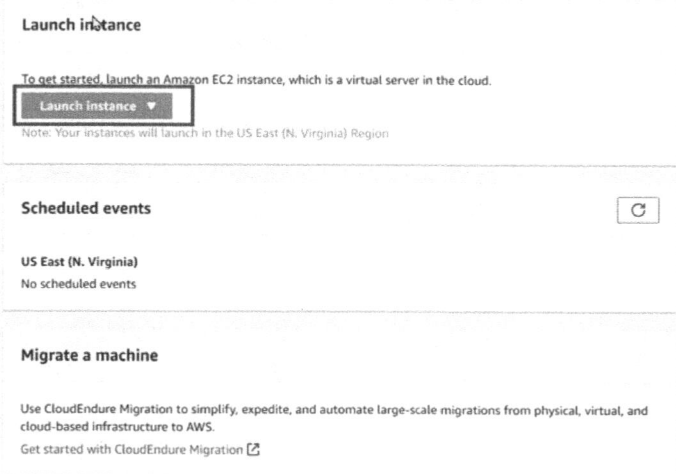

Figure 26

Below the launch instance button, you can see AZ's name where this instance will be created.

To open instance creation wizard-

5. Click Launch Instance.

This will give you a list of AMI (Amazon Machine Image). It is a template that has an operating system installed. Once the AMI is selected, it will launch/boot a Virtual Machine with a selected operating system. Take a look at the list of AMI offered by Amazon.

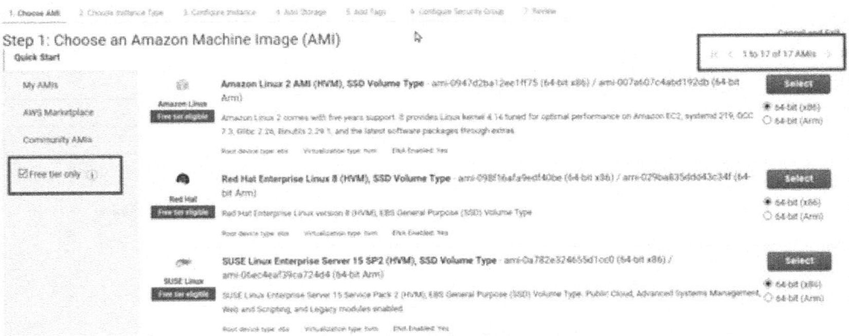

Figure 27

The filtration is based on Free Tier AMI only, Amazon has more than a dozen of it.

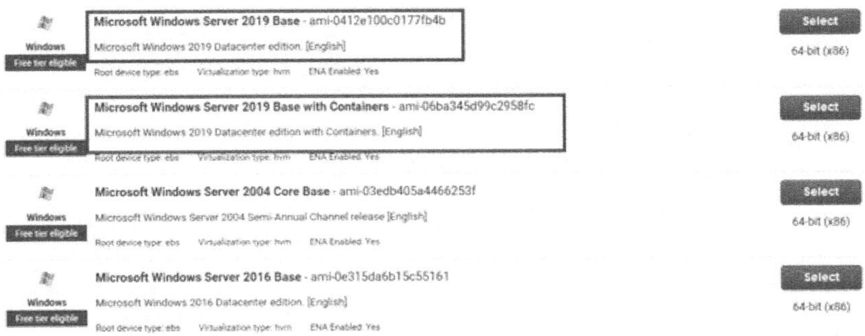

Figure 28

It offers some windows VM images as well. Have a look at the highlighted area. It is the image number. Every AMI has a unique number associated with it. This AMI number will be utilized in IaC (Infrastructure as Code), which means when you are creating an EC2 instance using API, these AMI numbers will be needed. Once you have selected AMI, it displays the instant type, which means what type of hardware it will be associated with. You can see t2.micro is eligible for the free tier instance.

6. On the Instance type page, select **Review and Launch** for quick launch.

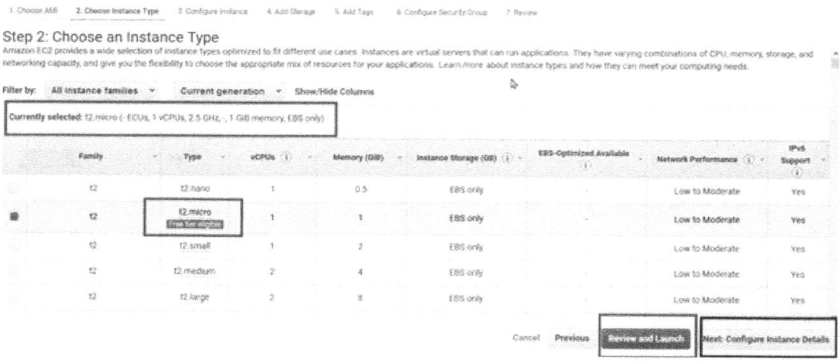

Figure 29

You can review and launch this instance, and else you have to look into the instance details and launch it. Once you click **Review and Launch,** the following window is displayed on the screen:

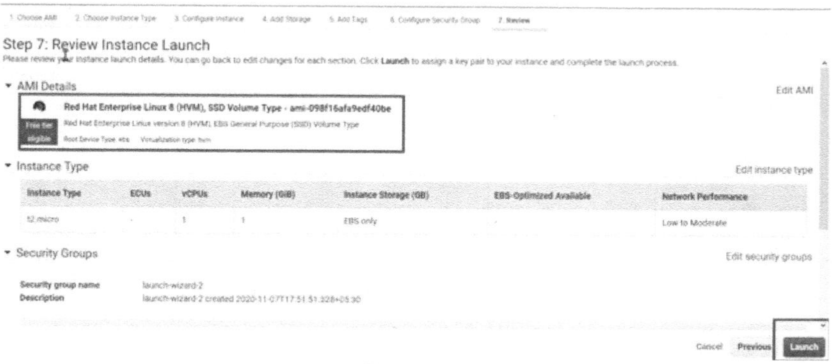

Figure 30

If you select the **Next-Configure Instance Details** button, you can see the detailed configuration.

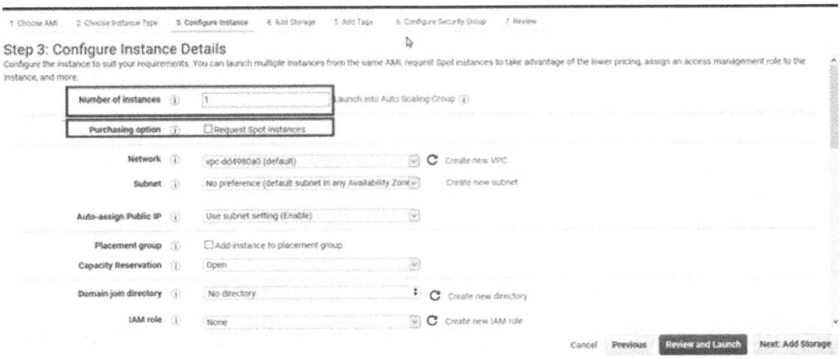

Figure 31

The next screenshot shows how to assign public IP (Elastic IP) address to this instance, which will be launched after review. If you have not selected any static IP, amazon will provide one IP address to this instance.

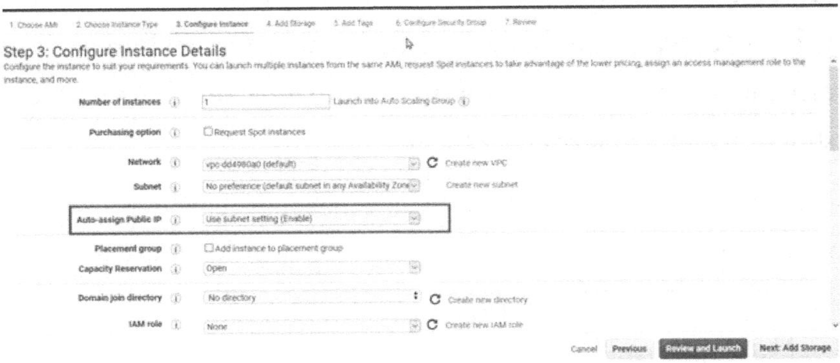

Figure 32

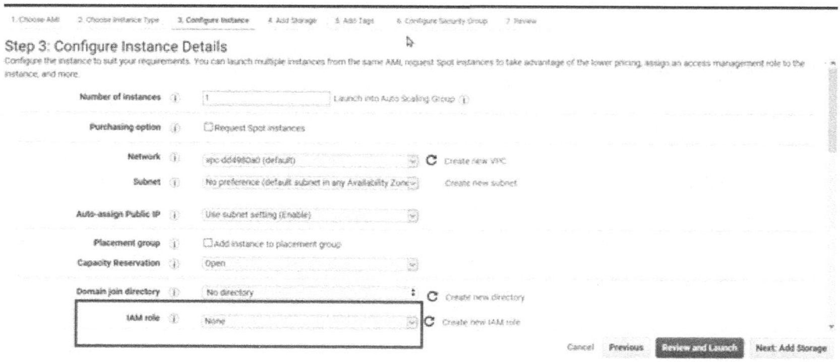

Figure 33

We are going to have it none, for now, we will see in detail about it. IAM role is user rights that are given for this user. The specific user can have any dashboard rights, or it can have only API access. These are other things that will be discussed in detail when we will look at the IAM section. You can provision up to 20 instances at a time. The above steps will help you to launch one instance. It has the facility to have a spot instance. (What is spot instance? or on-demand instance? we will see it in the next section.) When you will shut down the instance, by default it will stop it. However, you can change the behavior, you can terminate when the instance is shut down, it will terminate the instance.

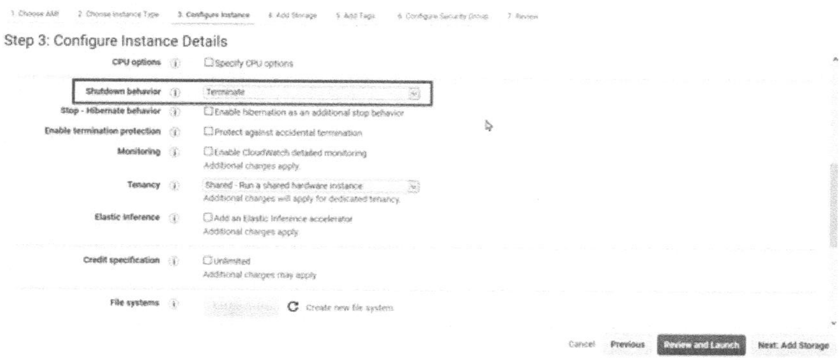

Figure 34

It has the option to protect it from accidental termination of this instance.

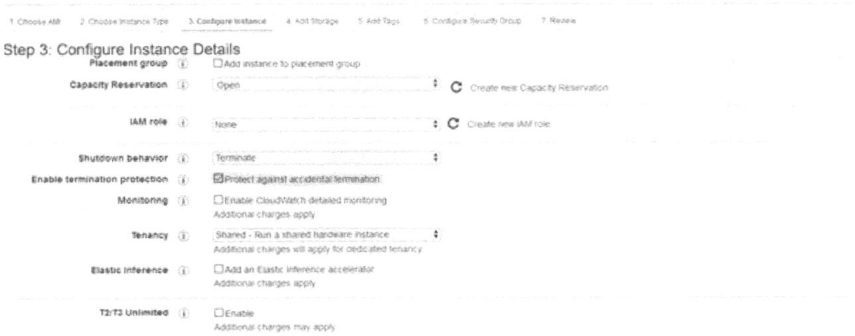

Figure 35

AWS provides basic monitoring free of cost. It is kept unchecked, as shown in the above figure. If your instance is critical for the business, select **Enable Cloudwatch detailed monitoring.**

Under tenancy, it is conveyed by the service provider that, for this instance, you need to have a dedicated server here, or a shared VM can also work. The default is shared hardware.

The next step is to add the storage page of this instance creation wizard.

Select the required storage at this stage.

Figure 36

When such type of EC2 instance increased, you may get confused about which instance belongs to what application. In the Add tag section, it can be searched. In the below figure, you can see the tag "webserver."

Figure 37

Go to the **Configure Security Group** section, where you have to select the user restrictions. It will select the default security group, which is created in default VPC, as shown in the below figure.

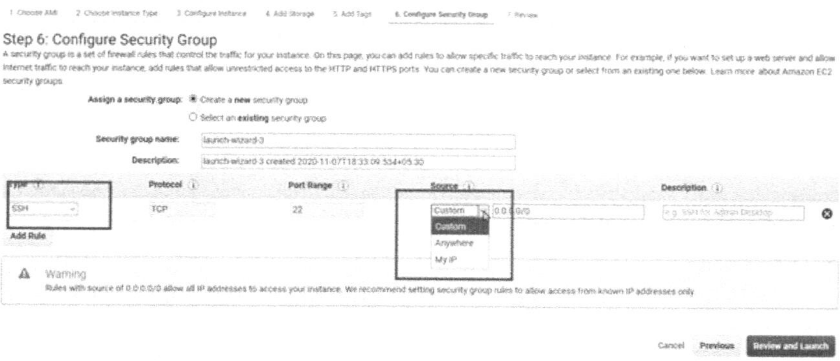

Figure 38

The network section gives a list of VPCs available on our platform. Select an already existing VPC. You can also create a new VPC.

> **Note** On the page of Configure Security Group, you can create a new VPC and security group. (In detail, we will observe it in the next section.).

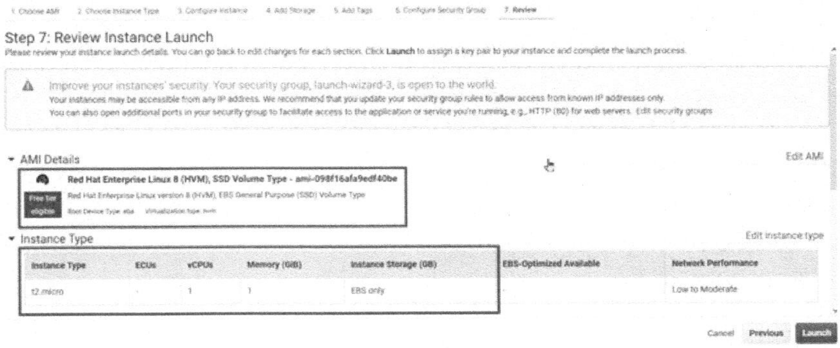

Figure 39

Note Make sure that you have reviewed what you have selected before launch.

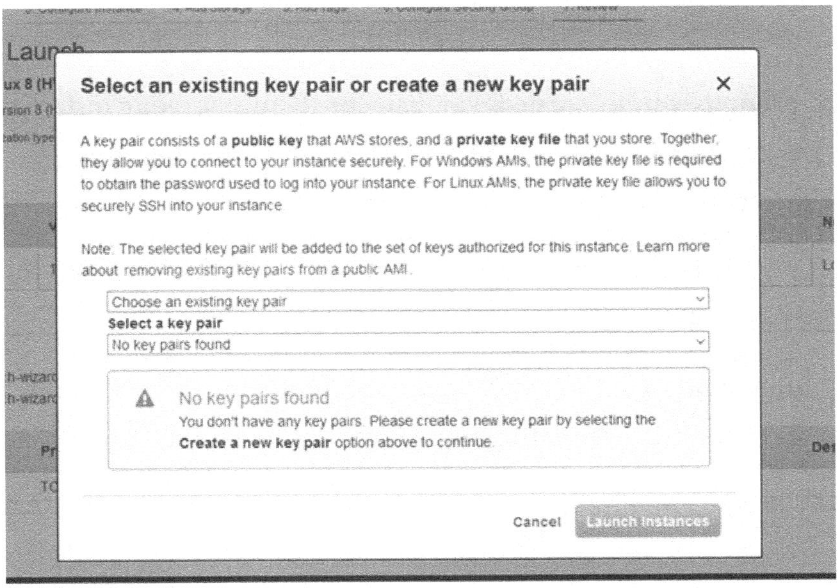

Figure 40

To create a new key pair, follow the procedure given below:

1. Type the name of your key.

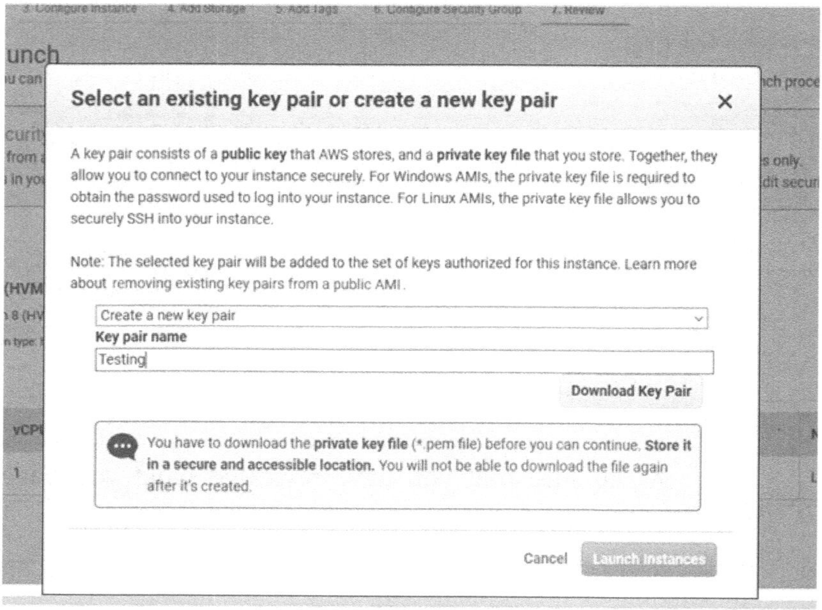

Figure 41

It prompts you to create a key pair for login into your instance. The key pair is a set of public-private keys. Using these keys, you can access instances through Amazon CLI from the client.

A private key is stored. For instance, AWS asks to download the private key.

Important	The key is very important. Make sure that it is stored in a safe location. In case it is lost, you will not be able to download it again.

2. Download it and save it at a secured location.
3. Download .pem file, launch instance will be enabled.

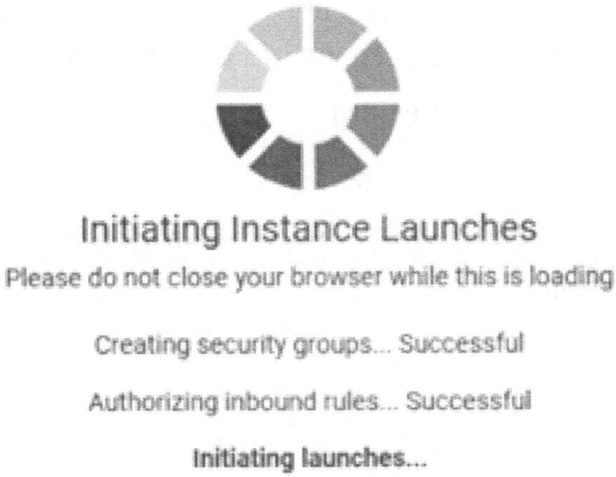

Figure 42

Here is the final message that your instance is configured.

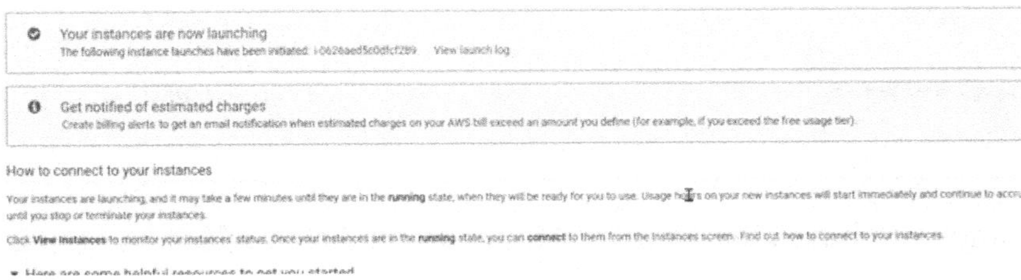

Figure 43

Let us see the status in the instance list on the instance page. This is how details are listed on the instance page.

- The status of the instance is running.
- All checks are passed by it.
- It is being assigned one Private IP address like 172.xxx.xxx xxx.
- This instance got one Public IP address as well, which is like 54.xxx.xxx.xx, still you can see the Elastic IP is an empty one.

As you have seen correctly, the public IP is a temporary one; with an instance restart, it might change. Elastic IP is a Static IP address that will be assigned to this instance.

In the past year, Amazon had only a private IP address. Now it is allocating one public address till you can assign elastic IP. It helps in the migration of servers.

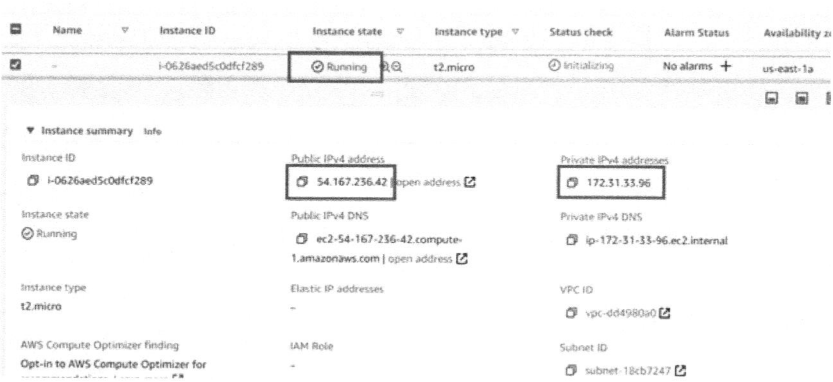

Figure 44

Since you have created one instance which is has a Red Hat Linux operating system installed on this server. A couple of years back, you had to assign Elastic IP (EIP); elastic IP is static IP that will be assigned to this server. To access this instance, now, you do not need to assign an EIP. You can use the Public IP assigned to connect to this instance.

Lab 2-Procedure to connect to an EC2 Instance

Since this is a Linux instance, let us open the putty session to connect the EC2 instance. The temporary public IP address assigned to this instance is 54.xxx.xxx.xx.

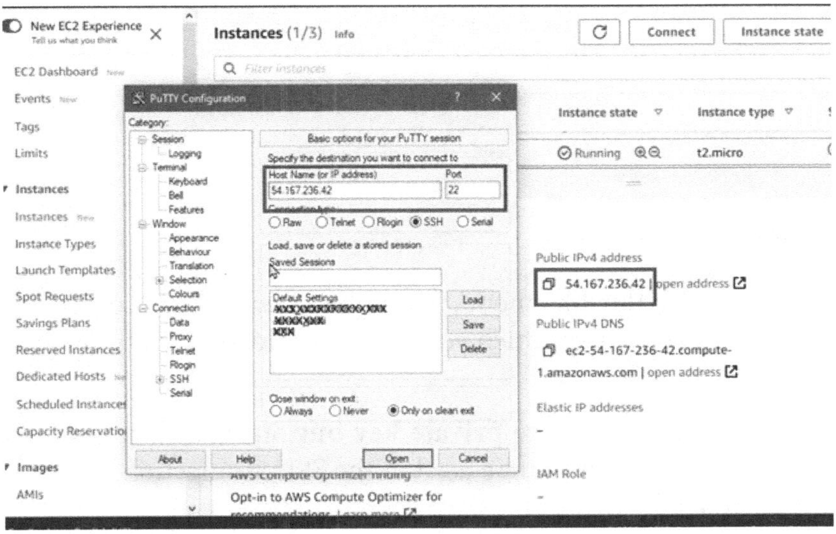

Figure 45

You may have noticed that till now, we have not created any user, nor credentials are shared while creating this instance. Every Linux system has one default user called EC2-user. Add your private key in putty for a secure connection.

1. Convert your .pem file to Putty Private Key (PPK). So, it will be used in putty to connect to the instance.

When you have installed putty from the Internet, it installs PuttyGen with it. Open it from the file menu.

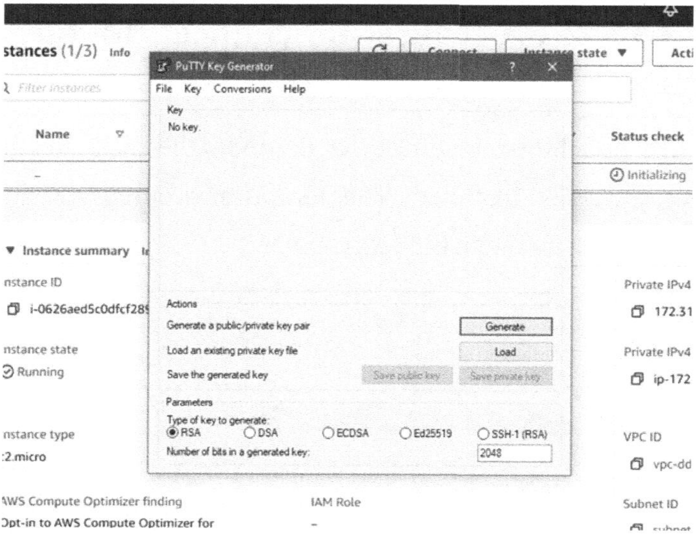

Figure 46

2. On the file menu, load the private key. Locate the private key which you have downloaded while creating the instance.

3. Click the **Save private key button**. It will save a .ppk file, which can be used in the SSH connection.

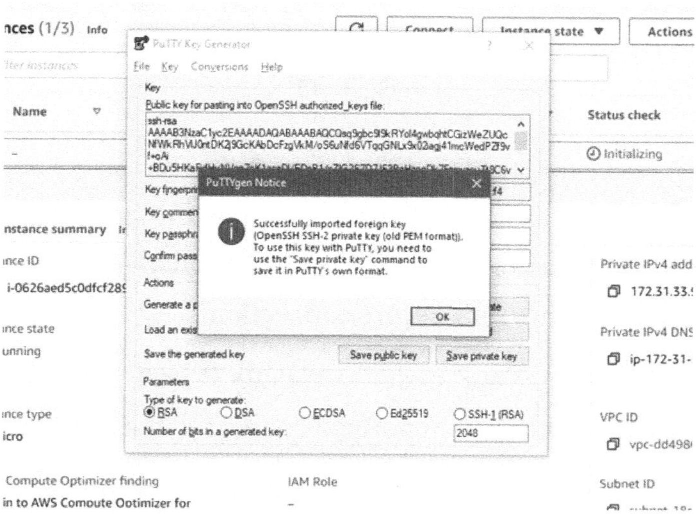

Figure 47

4. On the category, click the **SSH** menu and then select the **Auth** section.

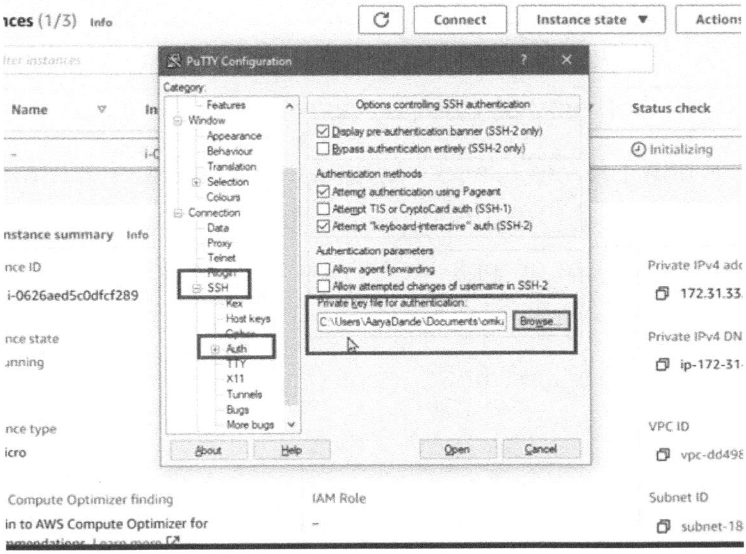

Figure 48

5. Using Puttygen, convert the .pem file from AWS to PPK.

6. Add your private key in .ppk (putty private key) format.

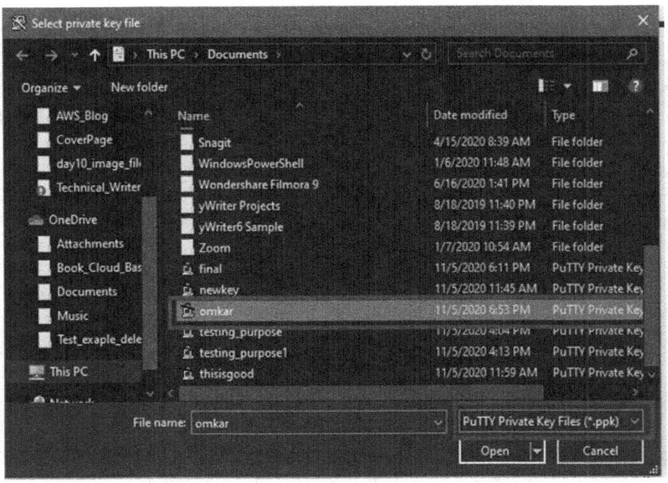

Figure 49

Note

> Add your private key in .ppk (putty private key) format. You will need to convert the pem file from AWS to ppk using puttygen.

7. Click on **Open**. Using ec2-user, a default user, log in to this server by using the given IP address.

This is how you can connect to the EC2 server using putty. This needs you should have this .pem or ppk file. But it is not safe to send this .pem or .ppk file to your resources to access these instances.

So next lab, we will see how to access instances by using the key.

Lab 3-Procedure to connect to an EC2 with key

1. First login with .ppk file to the EC2 instance using ec2-user
2. Sudo to root user, by sudo su command

3. The first thing you should do is set a password for the root user. Using the following command

   passwd

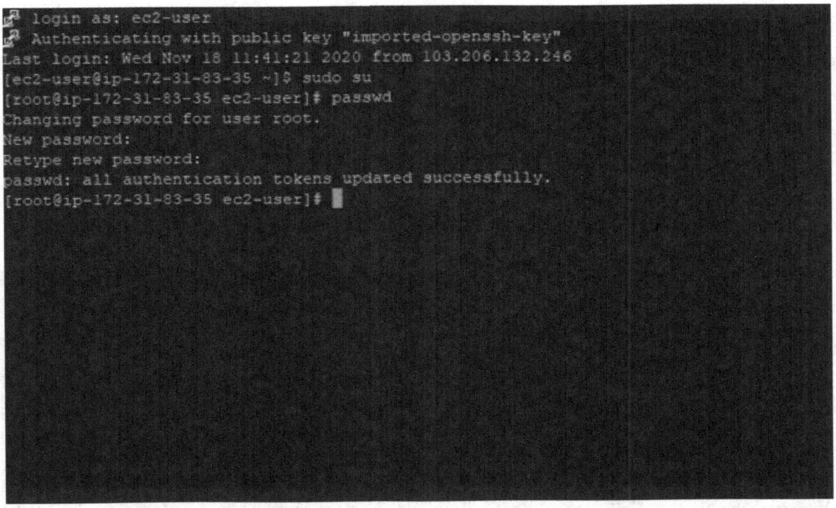

4. Add one user using command useradd and change it's password as follows

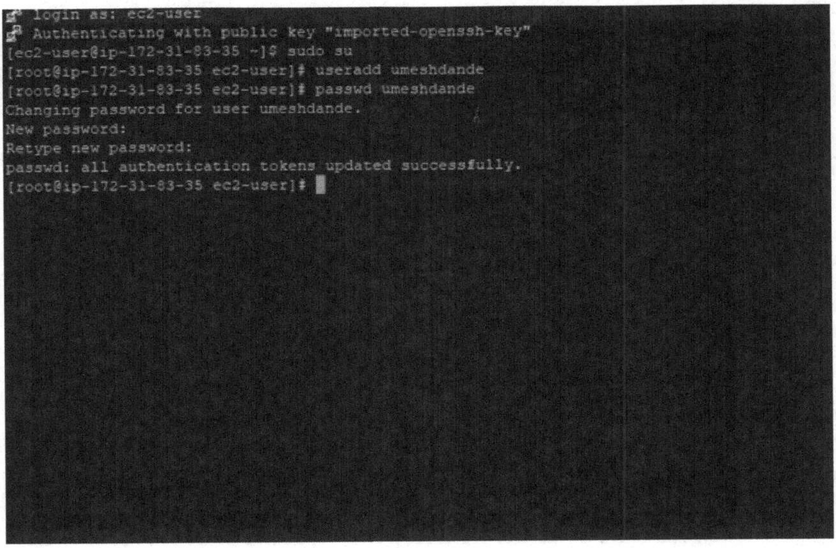

5. Add this user to sudo user group using the following command

   usermod –aG wheel umeshdande

6. Now we have to restrict ec2-user from login. And this new user should use a password for logging (ssh) to the system. Open following file sshd_config from root login using this command

   vi /etc/ssh/sshd_config

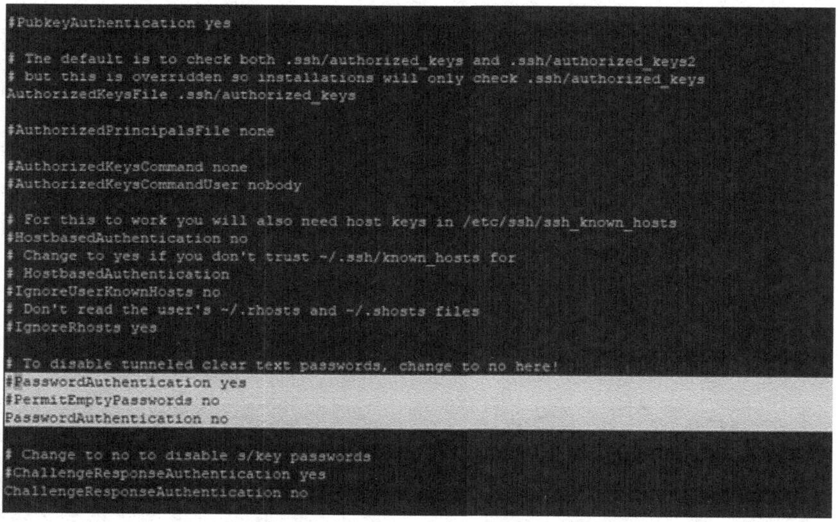

```
#PubkeyAuthentication yes

# The default is to check both .ssh/authorized_keys and .ssh/authorized_keys2
# but this is overridden so installations will only check .ssh/authorized_keys
AuthorizedKeysFile .ssh/authorized_keys

#AuthorizedPrincipalsFile none

#AuthorizedKeysCommand none
#AuthorizedKeysCommandUser nobody

# For this to work you will also need host keys in /etc/ssh/ssh_known_hosts
#HostbasedAuthentication no
# Change to yes if you don't trust ~/.ssh/known_hosts for
# HostbasedAuthentication
#IgnoreUserKnownHosts no
# Don't read the user's ~/.rhosts and ~/.shosts files
#IgnoreRhosts yes

# To disable tunneled clear text passwords, change to no here!
#PasswordAuthentication yes
#PermitEmptyPasswords no
PasswordAuthentication no

# Change to no to disable s/key passwords
#ChallengeResponseAuthentication yes
ChallengeResponseAuthentication no
```

7. Press I for edit mode. Replace no with yes, for an uncommented line.

8. Use the following command to restart the sshd service. Close window open new one

   systemctl restart sshd

9. Open the putty without using .ppk file. Try to login using ec2-user. Now it will ask for a password. When .ppk file is used in the putt, system will never prompt for a password.

10. Now close it and try to login using a new user created by root. After successful login, change to root, using sudo su command as follows.

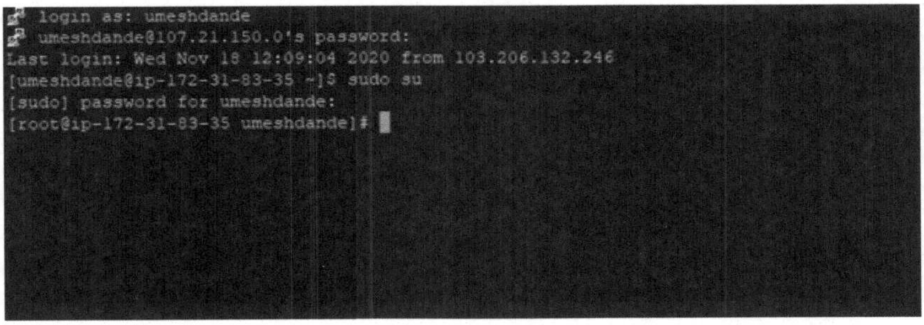

Now you can hand over this instance to any other user for utilization. If something goes wrong, you can use .ppk file to restore the login and all. These are the most important things as per security purposes.

> **Note**
>
> When you are adding a regular user to SSH group, different Linux flavor has other groups where this user should be added.
>
> Redhat - usermod -aG wheel your_user_id
>
> Ubuntu – usermod –aG sudo your_user_id

Do practice of these labs, lets meet on next day with IAM management studies.

♦ ♦

Day 4
Lab -1

CHAPTER *Four*

Identity and Access Management (IAM)

CHAPTER POINTS

- **How are users created in the AWS cloud?**
- **What level of security can be provided for user authentication?**
- **How are rights provided to the user?**
- **What is the best practice needs to be followed?**

4.1 Introduction to Identity and Access Management

In Amazon Web Services, it stands for Identity and Access Management (IAM).

AWS IAM provides identity management proficiencies for AWS customers. This is done by empowering IT administrators to control which users have the authorization to access different AWS resources and the type of activities they can accomplish.

AWS IAM controls three virtual objects for handling identities and access: Users, Groups, and Permissions.

- **Users:** It symbolizes real AWS customers and is used to validate distinct user identities and to provide access.
- **Groups:** It is a collection of users, which makes it easy for admins to control multiple users at once.
- **Permission:** It authorizes which AWS resources have a specific user or a set of users that have consented to access and the actions they can perform.

If you need to build this identity and access management, it is necessary to initially create the AWS account. It is better to start with a single sign-in type of identity; this specific identity is named as the root-user. This user has full rights to perform any operation in the AWS cloud. Best practice suggests creating another user for day to operations of these AWS accounts. Root-id should not be disclosed to more than a couple of users. It should be shared with only responsible people.

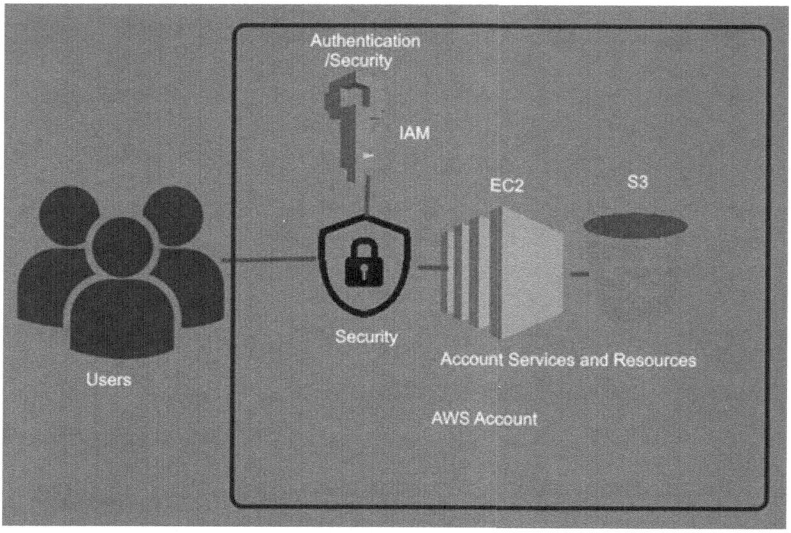

Figure 50

Following are certain essential features of AWS

- **Shared access to your AWS account**: You have the facility to grant others access to resources in your account without sharing your password. For example, with an access key, the resource can be accessed by the respective API.
- **Detail (granular) permissions**: Each user can have different permission. One user can have full access to EC2, S3, and Database. Others can have just read-only permission to S3 files, while individual users have only permission for billing.
- **Secure access to the application that runs on EC2**: If one of the applications is hosted on an EC2 instance still you can permit specific S3 bucket access or a couple of dynamo table access only. It adds one more layer of entry for security purposes.

- **Multi-factor authentication:** Since it is a cloud, user and password credentials might be cracked over the Internet. So it provides MFA; you can have an app or device which generates code that will be additionally used to authenticate.
- **Free secure way of authentication:** AWS Security Token Service (AWS STS) and IAM are the services offered free of cost; no additional fee is charged for it.

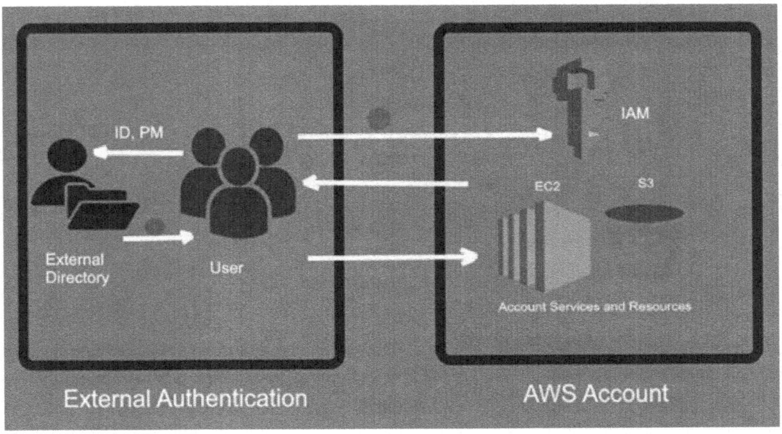

Figure 51

4.2 AWS IAM Best Practises

AWS IAM best practices help to perform specific comparative audits to remove all the idle users and IDs. This type of audit is performed to secure the AWS resources for assured AWS identities and Access Management Service (IAM).

Some of AWS IAM best practices are as follows:

- It is advised not to use root-users frequently; MFA should be enabled for it.
- Create individual IAM for a different user.

- Use AWS defined policies frequently for assigning the permissions since these are designed carefully.
- It is advisable to create a group by adding to the group assign permissions to IAM users.
- Try to grant the least privilege to the end-user.
- A periodic review of access levels should be done.
- Strong password policies should be set for the dashboard user.

Lab 1-Procedure to Create User and Group

These are the following type of ways for user creation in AWS:

- IAM (Console)
- IAM (AWS CLI)
- IAM (AWS API)

Creating Console User

Sign-in to the AWS account and open the IAM Dashboard

1. Log-in to the **AWS account**, open the **IAM Dashboard**.
2. On the navigation pane, select **Users** and then select **Add User**.

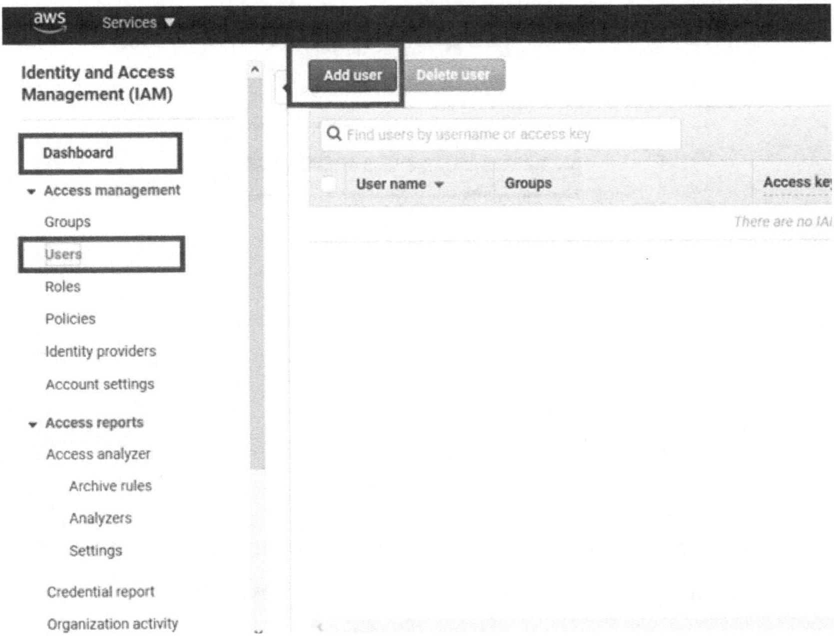

Figure 52

3. Type the user name for the new user. This is the sign-in name for AWS.

> **Note**
> If you want to add multiple users at the same time, select **Add Another User** and type their user names. You can add up to 10 users at one time.

4. Select the type of access this set of users will have. You can select programmatic access, access to the AWS Management Console, or both.

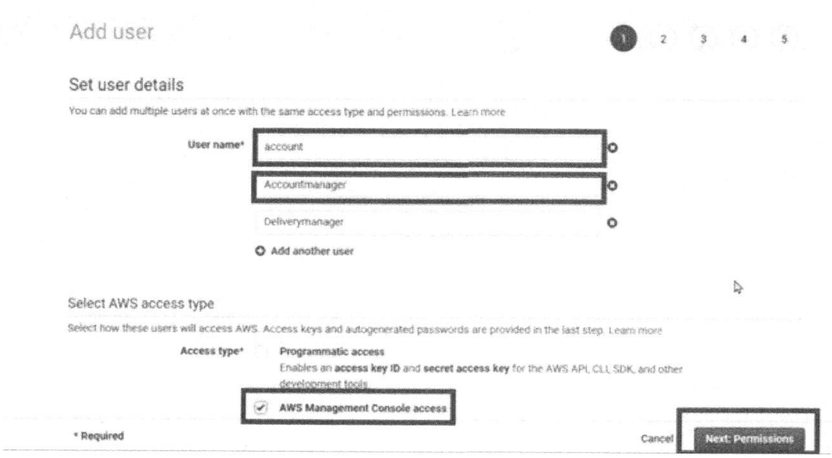

Figure 53

5. On the set permissions page, specify how you want to assign permissions to this set of new users.

Select one of the following options:

- Add user to group
- Copy permission from the existing group
- Attach existing policies directly to the user.
- Billing section (if you want to create a user who wants to see the only billing section by permitting to console.)

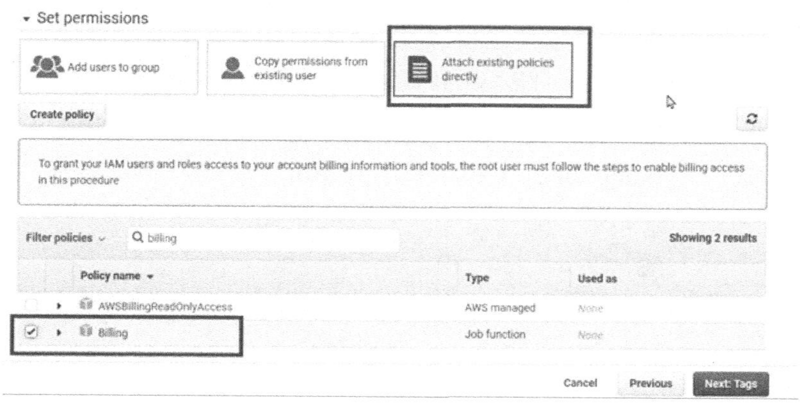

Figure 54

6. Add tags to search these users.

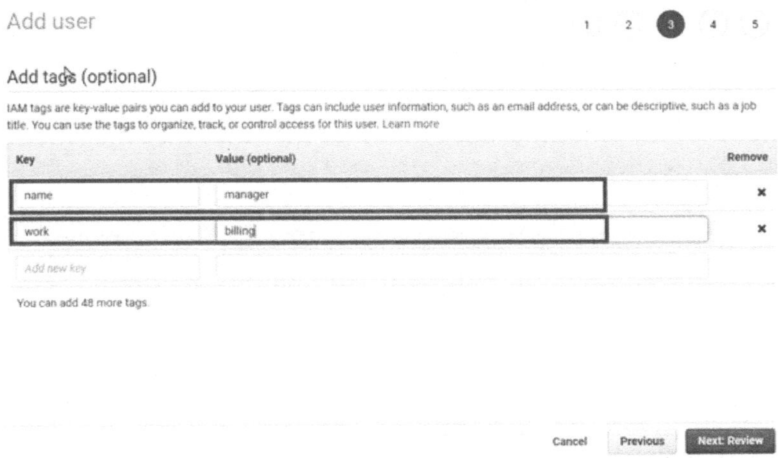

Figure 55

7. Review what has been added to create these users.

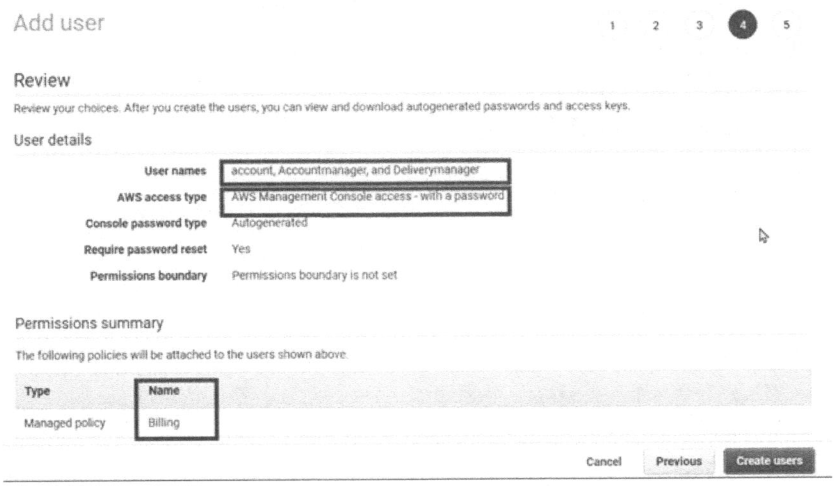

Figure 56

Since we have created multiple users with an auto-generated password facility, AWS provides the facility to store it, mail it, and show it here in the dashboard itself. Users need to change it after the first log-in.

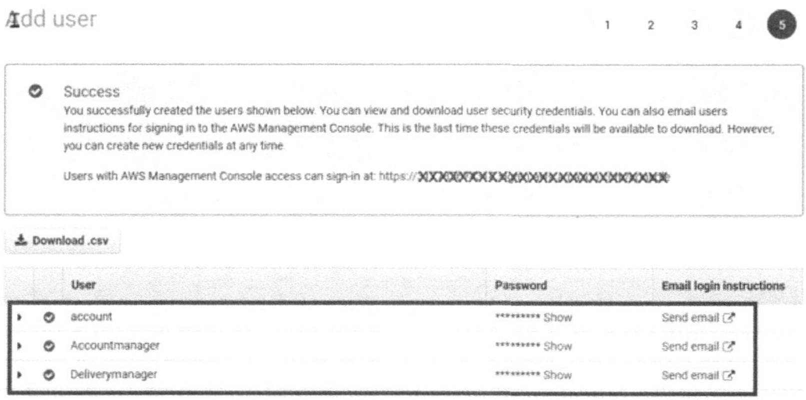

Figure 57

Umesh Tips

The user's password is not included in the generated email. You must provide them to the customer in a way that complies with your organization's security guidelines.

Creating AWS CLI User

1. Create a user.

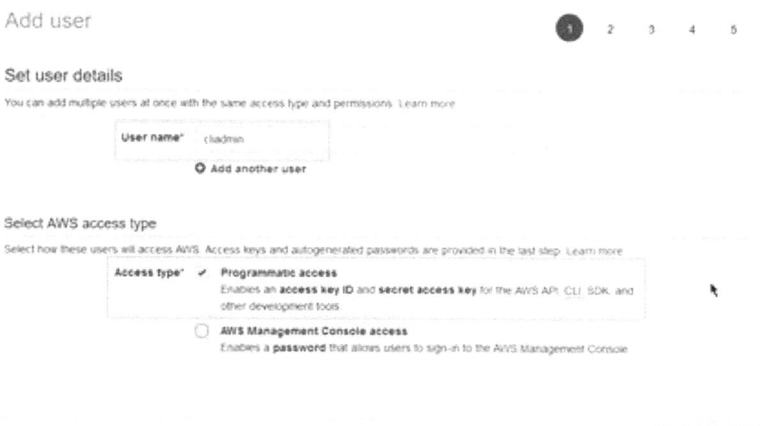

Figure 58

2. Give the user programmatic access. This requires access keys.

- AWS IAM create-access-key.

When configuring AWS CLI, you need to add these two keys

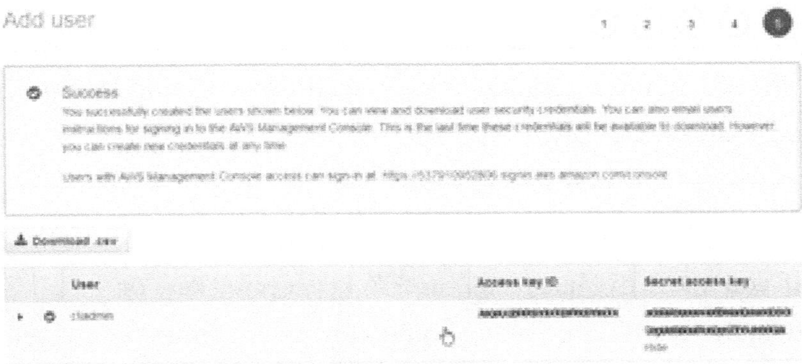

Figure 59

Then you can execute the command from CLI, check it like this.

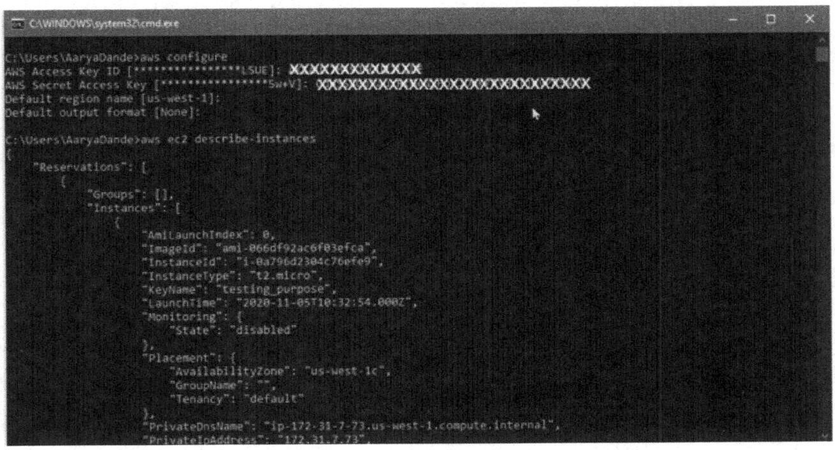

Figure 60

This is how you will have to configure the AWS CLI. When you hit the command AWS configure, it will ask for Access Key ID. The AWS Secret Access Key will ask to give you default regain so as it will execute the command for that regain. Let us configure the AWS CLI and see how the command executes and see the output.

Creating AWS API User

The procedure is the same as CLI user creation; the only usage is different. While accessing data using API, you should submit the access and secret key.

Umesh Tips

If you want to change the access key, secret key, or default regain name, you should run AWS configure command. It gives the option to change these things.

We have seen two words, "IAM" and "AMI" since it is a bit confusing. So let us discuss these over here

IAM (Identity and Access Management)	AMI (Amazon Machine Images)
It is a service provided by Amazon for authentication purposes.This service helps you to create users for accessing cloud resources.	It is Virtual Machine with a specific operating system.
It is related to the security of the cloud, it is attached to the security group which is defined for accessing cloud resources.	It is related to Virtual Machine. This is an image of a machine by using it, an EC2 instance can be created.

IAM (Identity and Access Management)	AMI (Amazon Machine Images)
It is a fre e service provided by Amazon.	It has both free and paid images available.
Users created by this service is a global one. It is not restricted to any region or available zone.	It is the availability zone (AZ) dependent. The image name/number which is there in one zone, will not be the same in other zones.

Difference between Snapshot and AMI

Topic	Snapshot of EC2	AMI (Amazon Machine Image)
Characteristic	It is a snapshot of the existing EC2 instance.	It is a type of template created for creating a new EC2 instance.
Purpose	Snapshot/ Backup of exiting EC2 instance.	These are images that havean operating system installed.
Space Required	It needs space to save the snapshot of an instance.	No user space is used for these images.

This is very good going, so you know how to create user in AWS. Do create couple of users, check E-mail sent by Amazon and other details. Lets meet on next day, we will discuss networking in AWS

♦ ♦

Day 5
Lab -1

CHAPTER *Five*

Network Setup in Cloud

CHAPTER POINTS

- **How is the network set up in the cloud?**
- **How are routes configured into the AWS cloud?**
- **Does this have a routing table, subnet mask?**
- **Does it have Gateway? How is Gateway configured in the cloud?**
- **What is elastic load balancing?**
- **What is the cloud front?**

5.1 Introduction to Networking and Configuration

Amazon cloud shares many things that are common between cloud and in-premises set-up. Like you have a virtual server created on enterprise hardware, same with AWS, it has EC2 instance created as virtual servers.

Now comes the part of the network, in-premises you have switches, routers, and firewalls to define the access and restriction for a particular user. The following are some of the network-oriented services offered by AWS.

- Amazon Direct Connect links your local network to the AWS cloud and its resources. It is built over 1 GB to 10 GB ethernet fiber optic cable.
- Amazon Route 53 is the service to be required for domain resolution, domain name system (DNS).
- Amazon Virtual Private Clouds (VPC) is an arrangement that lets your resource securely isolated from others. It has everything that is defined in switches and routers.

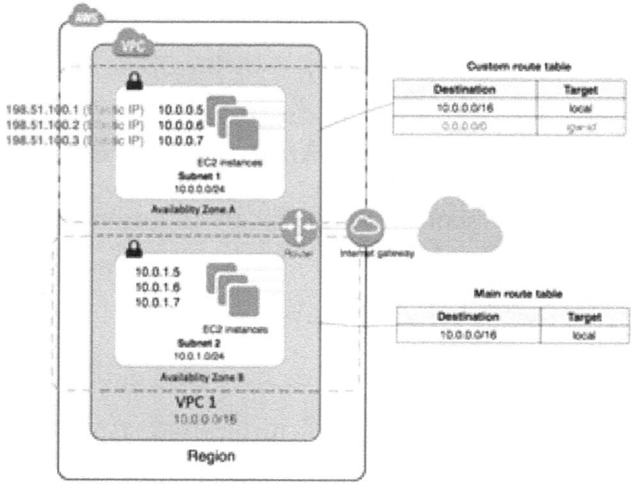

Figure 61

As you can see in the above figure, VPC is a virtual boundary for infrastructure, it can span across the availability zone but it is restricted to a region.

5.2 AWS Networking: Virtual Private Network (VPC)

Amazon Virtual Private Cloud (Amazon VPC) facilitates you to unveiling Amazon Web Services (AWS) resources into a virtual network that you have created. This virtual network closely looks like a traditional network that you may have controlled in the data center, with the remunerations of using the scalable infrastructure of AWS.

However, there is a similarity between in-premises network and VPC with some specific differences. One default VPC will be created for each and every account for every regain.

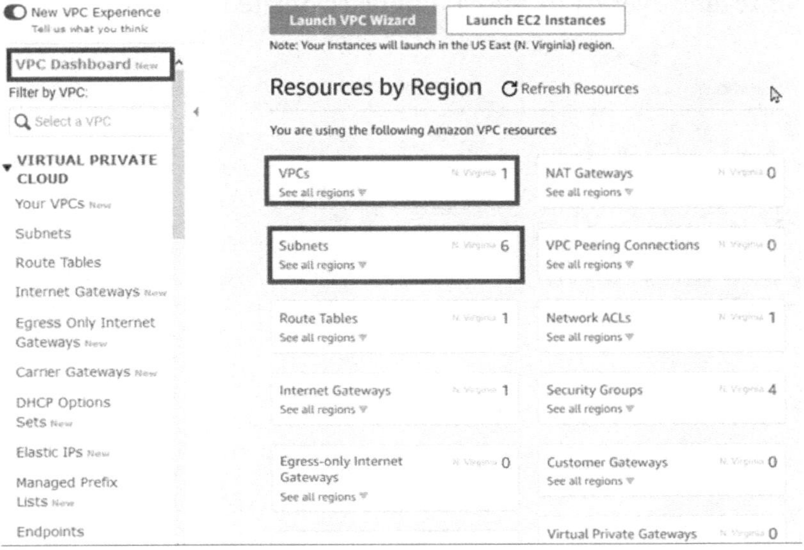

Figure 62

Umesh Tips

The subnet is AZ specific, one subnet can be spanned to one AZ.

Every regain has one subnet for one availability zone, a subnet can span across only one AZ. One regain can have multiple availability zones, so one regain can host multiple subnets under one VPC.

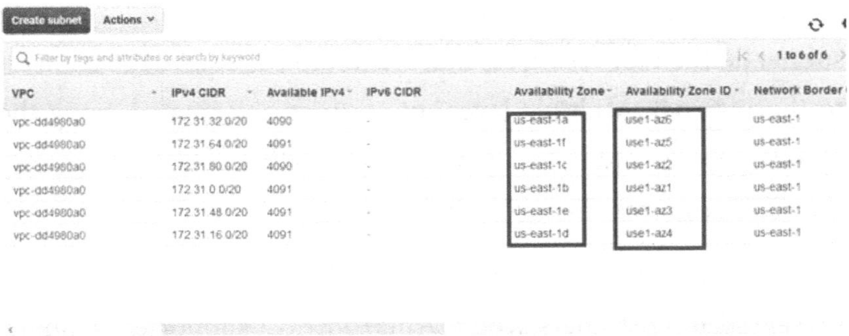

Figure 63

For regain, every VPC has a unique ID related to it.

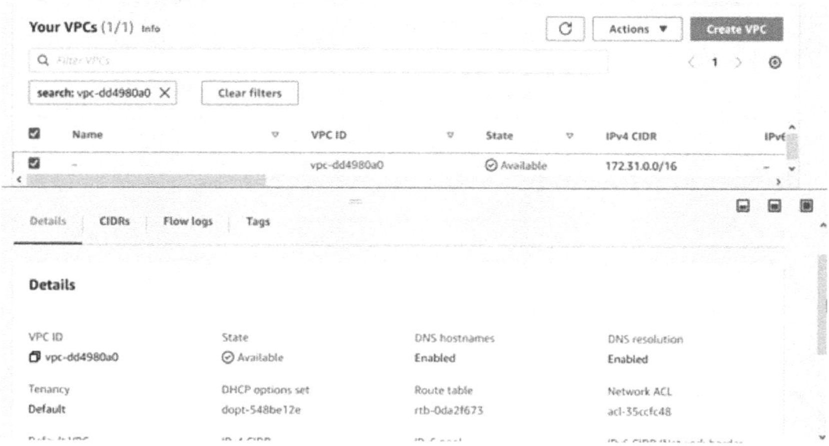

Figure 64

A virtual private cloud (VPC) is a virtual network committed to your AWS account. It is understandably isolated from other virtual networks in the AWS Cloud. You can introduce your AWS resources, such as EC2 instance into the created VPC. You can define an IP address range for the VPC, add associate security groups, subnets, and configure route tables.

A subnet is a range of IP addresses in your VPC. You can create AWS resources into a created subnet. Use a public subnet for resources that must be connected to the Internet and a private subnet defined for resources that are not to be required to connect to the Internet. Multiple layers of security are created using the security group and network access control lists (ACL) to protect the AWS resources in each subnet.

The first flat network release called EC2-Classic Platform was presented to customers where Amazon EC2 supported a single, flat network. Those earlier AWS accounts still support the EC2-

Classic platform with that they can launch instances into either EC2-Classic or a VPC. Accounts created after 2013-12-04 only support EC2-VPC.

By launching your instances into a VPC instead of EC2-Classic, you gain the ability to:

- A persistent IPv4 address can be assigned to your EC2 instance that persists across starts and stops.
- You have the choice of assigning IPv4 or IPv6 CIDR block to your VPC so as your that instances can have IPv6 IP addresses as well.
- It gives you the facility to assign multiple IPs to EC2 instances.
- You can define and attach one or more network interfaces to your instances.
- You can change the security group membership for your instances while they are running.
- You can control the outbound traffic from your instances (egress filtering) besides control the inbound traffic to instance (ingress filtering).
- You can add one more security layer by adding network access control lists (ACL).
- You can run instances on single-tenant hardware.

Now recently created account comes with a default VPC. One VPC is default created per regain. The default VPC has the assistance of the advanced structures provided by EC2-VPC and is equipped for you to use. If you have not created any VPC, the EC2 instance is by default created into this VPC, you do not require to specify any subnet for it. Amazon has made it simple, if you do not know how to create a VPC or have less knowledge of networking, you can use this default VPC to launch an EC2 Instance.

Regardless of having a default VPC, you can create/customize your VPC, which is called a non-default VPC. Subnet which is formed into this VPC is called non-default subnets.

Let us see the parts which are involved in VPC configurations. As our in-premises network set-up is there, it has lots of factors that are required to be understood before configuring a VPC.

Subnets: Subnets can be differentiated into two types, public subnet and private subnet. The subnet which drives traffic to the Internet gateway is known as a public subnet. For example, an application server that is open for the customer to access through the Internet, these servers are defined as the public subnet. Specific other servers that are connecting to the application server or backend servers are defined as the private subnet. This subnet traffic is routed to the Internet.

---

[2] egress filtering - is the practice of monitoring and potentially restricting the flow of information outbound from one network to another. Typically it is information from a private TCP/IP computer network to the Internet that is controlled.

[3] ingress filtering - is the practice of monitoring, controlling and restricting traffic entering a network with the objective of ensuring that only legitimate traffic is allowed to enter and that unauthorised or malicious traffic is prevented from doing so.

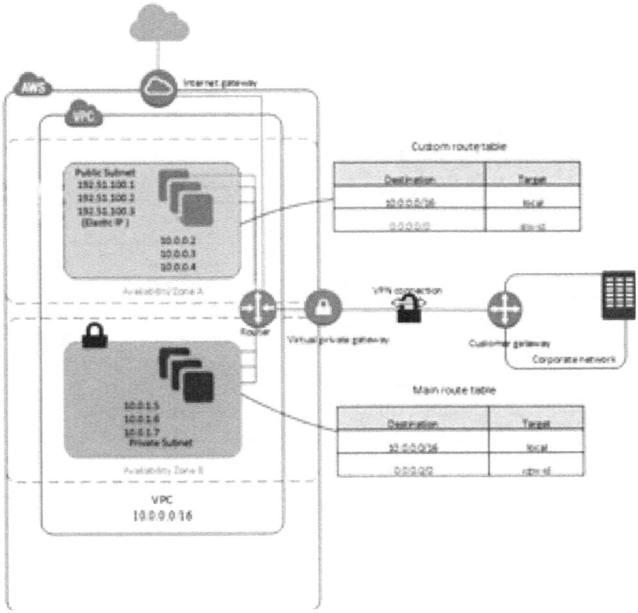

Figure 65

The above infrastructure architect has created two separate subnets. It is a public subnet which is 192.xx.xxx.x which is an elastic IP address. These servers can accept incoming traffic from the Internet. This subnet is connected to the Internet gateway. Whereas 10.x.x.x/16 is a private subnet that is connected to the VPG VPN gateway for connecting to the corporate office.

As we have discussed before, a subnet can span across a single availability zone. You can have multiple subnets within a VPC that can span to different availability zones. In short, one subnet to one AZ and one VPC to one regain (which might have more than one AZ's). The below image shows how the subnet is designed in VPC. It has a VPC, which is defined in a regain. 10.0.0.0/24 is a subnet defined in availability zone A and 10.0.1.0/24 is a subnet defined in availability zone B.

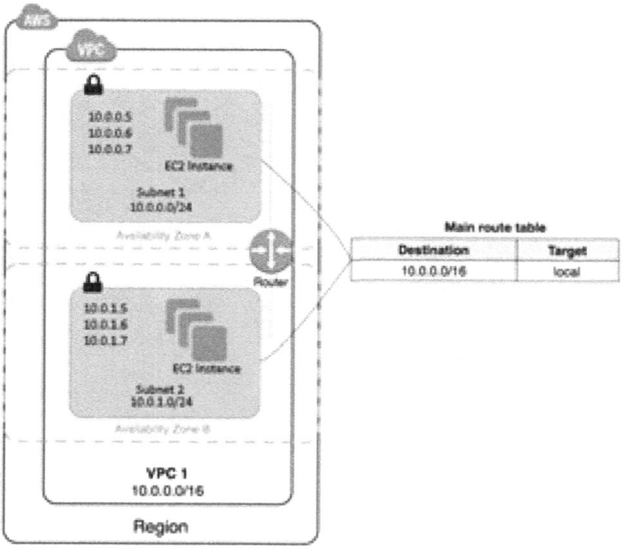

Figure 66

Regions and Availability Zones: AWS has isolated regions from each other. It is usually best to choose to regain that is geographically close to your office, it will reduce the network latency. Multiple availability zones are connected with low latency links in a regain.

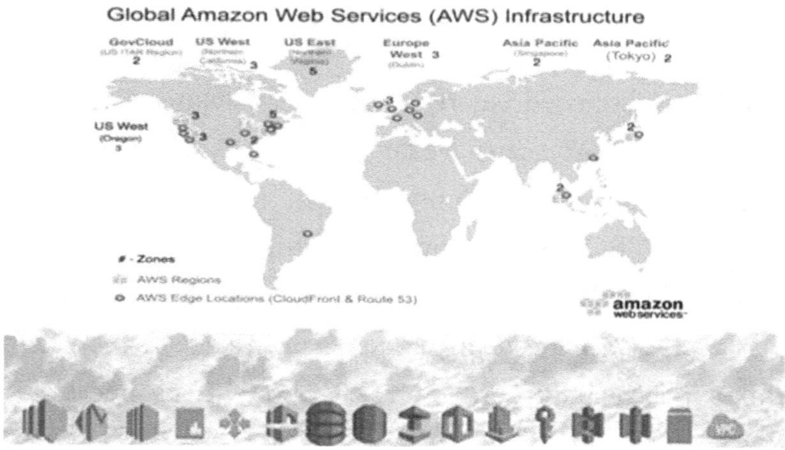

Figure 67

Security Groups and NACLs: AWS is a secured network. Security groups and NACLs are the two elements that play a great role in making it secure. These two are made up of certain rules written into it, to control the incoming and outgoing traffic. The security group works at the instance level, every EC2 instance is attached to one more security groups. While NACLs are the traffic rule defined at the subnet level.

The difference between the Security Groups and Network ACL is as follows:

Security Group	Network ACL
Supports allow rules only {by default all rules are denied} You cannot deny a certain IP address from establishing a connection.	**Supports allow and deny rules:** By denying rules it means, youcan explicitly deny a certain IP address to establish a connection. For example: Block IP address 192.168.0.2 from establishing a connection to an EC2 Instance.
Stateful: This means any changes applied to an incoming rule will be automatically applied to the outgoing rule. For example, If you allow an incoming port 80, the outgoing port 80 will be automatically opened.	**Stateless:** This means any changes applied to an incoming rule will not be applied to the outgoing rule. For example, if you allow an incoming port 80, you will also need to apply the rule for outgoing traffic.

<table>
<tr><th>Security Group</th><th>Network ACL</th></tr>
<tr><td>Security groups are tied to an instance.</td><td>Network ACL is tied to the subnet.</td></tr>
<tr><td>All rules in a security group are applied.</td><td>Rules are applied in their order (the rule with the lower number is gets processed first)
<table>
<tr><th>Rule # (Order number)</th><th>Type</th><th>Protocol</th><th>Port Range</th><th>Source</th><th>Allow/ Deny</th></tr>
<tr><td>100</td><td>HTTP (80)</td><td>TCP(6)</td><td>80</td><td>0.0.0.0/0</td><td>ALLOW</td></tr>
<tr><td>200</td><td>TCP (6)</td><td>TCP(6)</td><td>20</td><td>0.0.0.0/0</td><td>DENY</td></tr>
</table></td></tr>
<tr><td>First Layer of Defense</td><td>Second Layer of the defense</td></tr>
<tr><td>It is the Firewall of EC2 Instance.</td><td>Is the Firewall of the Subnet</td></tr>
<tr><td>Security groups are used in many cases. For example, they are restricting inbound traffic of an EC2 instance from the only load balancer.</td><td>The same thing applies to Network ACL</td></tr>
</table>

Internet Gateways: An Internet Gateway (IGW) can be created as soon as you have created VPC, and it is attached to this VPC. As the name suggests, it is to connect resources within VPC to the

[4]Means Security Group protection is till EC2 and NACLS are for subnet mask (ALL EC2 and other component in that subnet mask)

Internet. If you are setting up an instance, create it with a security group that allows the minimum possible amount of traffic, like 22 (SSH) ports open from your source IP.

Route Tables: These are rules which say that **A** IP address traffic should go to **B** (IGW) for the Internet. If you have different subnets that need to talk to each other, you will have to add entries into the routing table.

You will get to know more about it in the labs, which will be followed by this section.

> **Umesh Tips**
>
> Security Groups are stateful and NACLs are stateless.

Lab 1-Procedure to Create VPC

1. Log-in to AWS Account.
2. Below Networking & Content Delivery, select VPC.

All the networking related options are listed below the Networking & Content Delivery.

If you have recently visited this menu, you can see VPC on the drop-down of history as shown in the below figure.

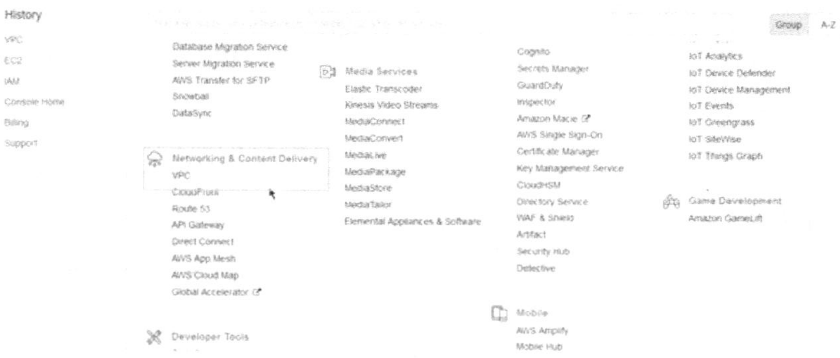

Figure 68

3. Click Launch VPC Wizard.

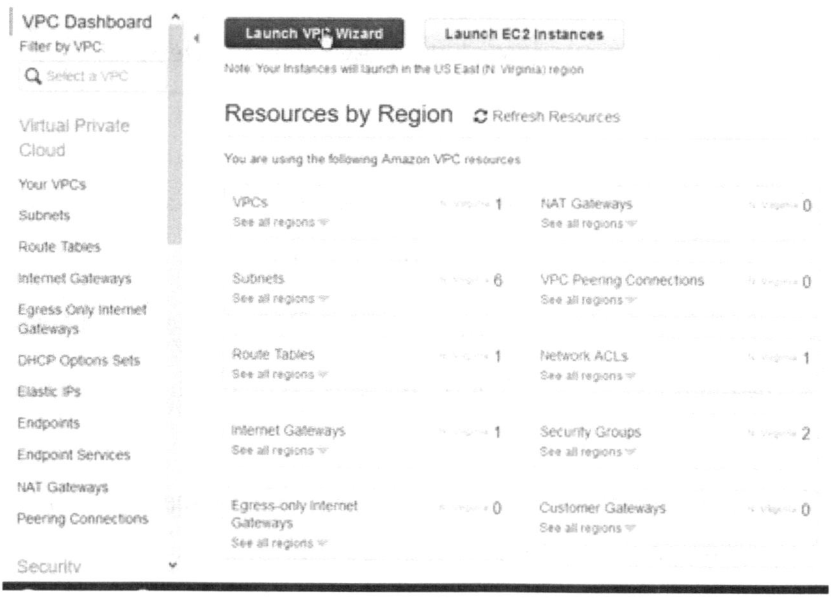

Figure 69

In Amazon, there are options to choose the specific type of VPC that you want to create.

- VPC with the single public subnet, these type of VPC are used for an application server and website

- VPC with the public and private subnet
- VPC with the public, private subnet with hardware VPN access
- VPC with private subnet and VPN access

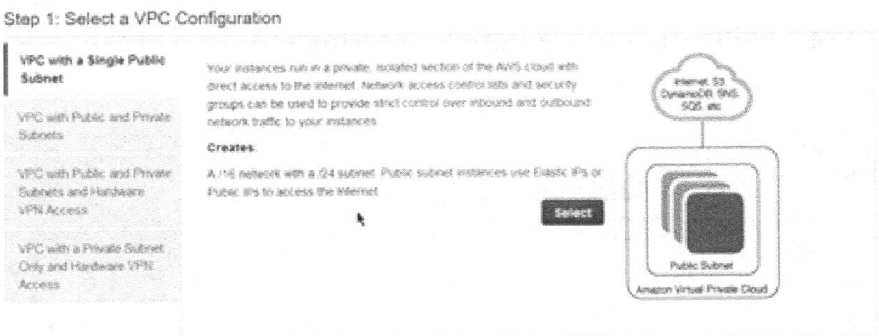

Figure 70

For this Lab, we will create VPC with the public, private subnet with VPN access.

Figure 71

For this lab, we have selected the IPv4 CIDR block of 10.0.0.0/16. One public network with 10.0.0.0/24 and a private network 10.0.1.0/24.

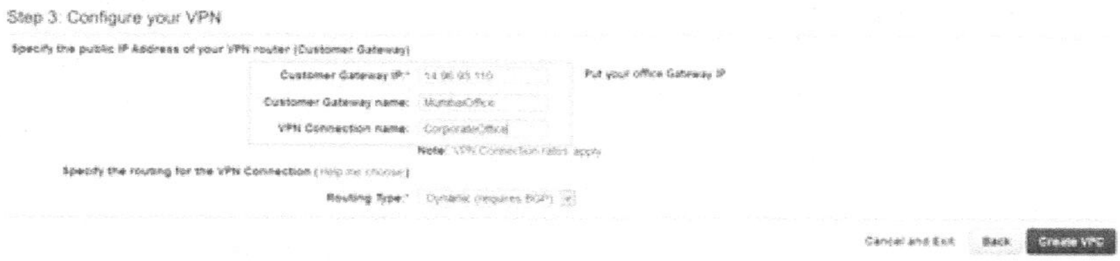

Figure 72

4. Fill in the required information and then click CreateVPC.

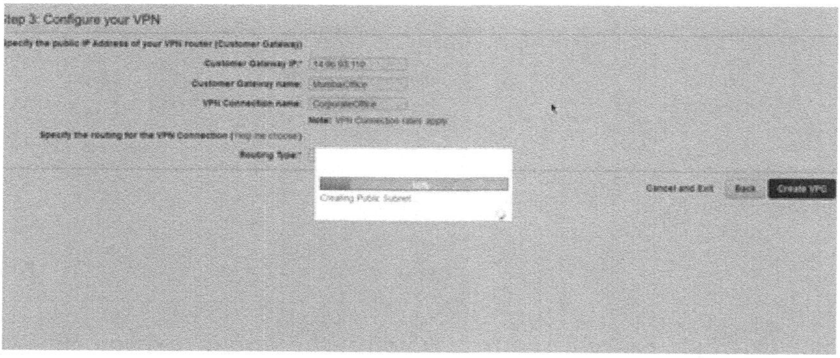

Figure 73

It will create all components requiring for setting this VPC.

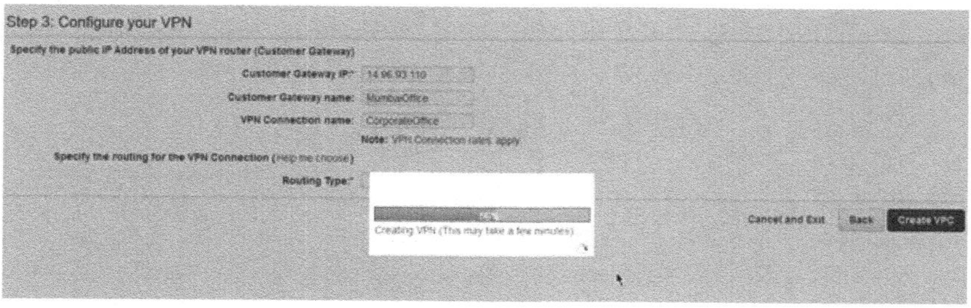

Figure 74

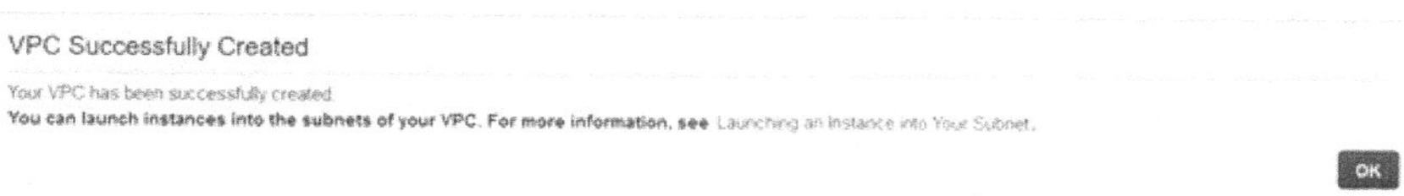

Figure 75

5.3 AWS Direct Connect

AWS direct is a connection dedicated link from local resources to AWS resources. It connects through 1gigabit to 10-gigabit Ethernet fiber-optic cable. You can form virtual interfaces straight to public AWS services (for example, to Amazon S3 or Amazon VPC), avoiding internet service providers in your network path. An AWS direct connect location offers access to AWS in the region with which it is linked. You can use a single connection in a public region or AWS GovCloud (US) to access public AWS services in all other public regions.

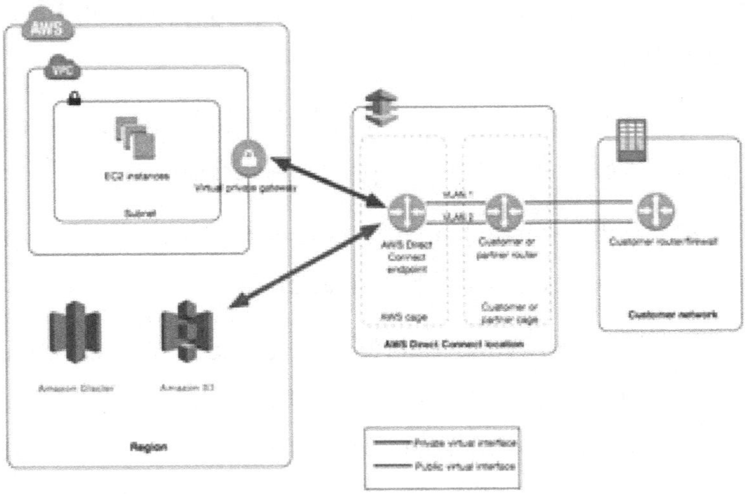

Figure 76

AWS direct has the following associated components with it.

Connections: Establish one connection between your premises to AWS regain. It is going to be a gigabit fiber network. There are two types of connections, namely, dedicated connection and hosted connection.

- Dedicated Connection: This is a dedicated connection

between single customers to AWS setup. Businesses can demand a dedicated connection over the AWS direct connect console, the CLI, or the API.

- Hosted Connection: This connection is provisioned by the AWS direct connect partner that has a physical ethernet connection. Businesses demand a hosted connection by communicating with a partner in the AWS direct connect partner program, who enables the connection.

Virtual Interfaces: There are three types of interfaces namely, a private virtual interface, a public virtual interface, and a transit virtual interface.

- Private virtual interface: It should be used to access an Amazon VPC using private IP addresses.
- Public virtual interface: It can access all AWS public services using public IP addresses.
- Transit virtual interface: It should be used to access one or more Amazon VPC transit gateways linked with direct connect gateways. You can use transit virtual interfaces with 1/2/5/10 Gbps AWS direct connect connections.

5.4 Amazon Route 53

If you want your customers to discover you, then you will need DNS routing. Route 53 provides the solution to this problem, it offers a highly scalable and available Domain Name System (DNS), domain name registration, and health checking web services.

The features of route 53 are as follows:

- **Resolver:** Get recursive DNS for your Amazon VPC and in-premises networks. It creates conditional forwarding rules and DNS endpoints, to resolve custom names mastered in Amazon Route 53 private hosted zones or your in-premises DNS servers.
- **Latency Based Routing:** Route end users to the AWS region that provides the lowest possible latency.
- **Geo DNS:** Route end users to a particular endpoint that you specify based on the end user's geographic location.
- **Private DNS for Amazon VPC:** Manage custom domain names for your internal AWS resources without exposing DNS data to the public Internet.
- **Health Checks and Monitoring:** Amazon Route 53 can observe the health and performance of your application as well as your web servers and other resources.
- **Cloud Front Zone Apex Support:** Once using Amazon CloudFront to provide your website content, people on your website can now access your site at the zone apex (or "root domain"). For example, your site can be retrieved as example.com in place of www.example.com.
- **Amazon ELB Integration:** Amazon Route 53 is integrated with Elastic Load Balancing (ELB).

5.5 Amazon CloudFront

It is a low latency service that delivers video, data, applications,

[5]DDoS- Distributed Denial of Service

and APIs to the worldwide customer with high transfer speed. It is a content delivery network (CDN). It transfers data within a developer-friendly environment. CloudFront works seamlessly with other services such as Amazon Shield and DDoS mitigation, S3 and Elastic Load balancer, and so on.

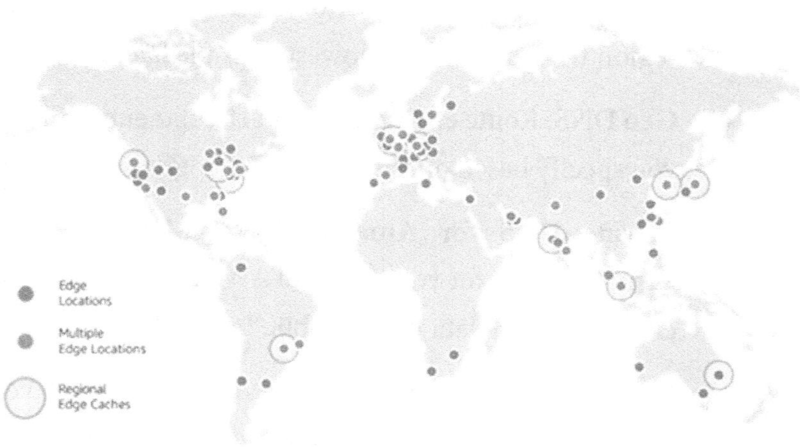

Figure 77

To deliver content to end-users with low latency, Amazon CloudFront uses a global network of 216 Points of Presence (205 Edge Locations and 11 Regional Edge Caches) across 42 countries in 84 cities.

Some of the features of Amazon CloudFront are as follows:

- **Protection against Network and Application Layer Attacks**: It works with AWS shield, AWS web application firewall (WAF), and route 53 to create layered security to stop attacks.
- **SSL/TLS Encryptions and HTTPS:** you can use AWS Certificate Manager (ACM) to create a custom SSL

certificate and deploy it to your CloudFront distribution for free.

- **Access Control:** The geo-restriction capability allows you to prevent users in specific geographic locations from accessing content that you are distributing through CloudFront.
- **Compliance:** CloudFront infrastructure and processes are all compliant with PCI-DSS Level 1 , HIPAA , and ISO 9001, ISO 27001, SOC (1, 2, and 3) to ensure the secure delivery of your most sensitive data.
- **Increase application availability:** By using Amazon CloudFront, the application can cache its content in CloudFront's edge locations worldwide and decrease the workload on your application server by only fetching content from the application server when needed. It will decrease the workload on your application server, which will help to increase the availability of your application.
- **Network optimization for optimal performance:** Since it will have cache content at the cloud front edge location, the network travel will be reduced, as cached content will be delivered from edge location only, which will optimize the network performance.

[6]PCI-DSS Level 1 - The Payment Card Industry Data Security Standard Level 1

[6]HIPAA - Covered entities and business associates are questioning whether and how they can take advantage of cloud computing while complying with regulations protecting the privacy and security of electronic protected health information

- **Dynamic or static content:** CloudFront caches the data in the edge locations to speed up the access of the website from the client. We wanted to access the static and dynamic contents using a single CloudFront endpoint. At the same time, static pages are cached while dynamic pages are spared from caching.
- **Full-featured APIs and DevOps Tools:** It provides a developer with a wide range of API to create, configure, and maintain your CloudFront distribution. With that, developers have access to a number of tools such as AWS CloudFormation, CodeDeploy, CodeCommit, and AWS SDKs to configure and arrange their loads with Amazon CloudFront.
- **Edge behaviors:** CloudFront can be organized with several behaviors. Administers know how CloudFront will process the request and what features will be functional. It will take control of exactly how CloudFront caches and communicates with the application server, customize what headers and metadata are forwarded to the application server, create content variants with flexible cache-key manipulation. It supports various compression modes and other customizations.
- **Pay-as-you-go publicly available pricing and committed-traffic private pricing:** For the use of CloudFront you don't need to make an upfront payment, it is being accumulated in pay-as-you-go. No minimal cost will be changed as well.

- **Free data Transfer between AWS cloud services and Amazon CloudFront:** No charges will be applied for data transfer from your application server to edge location.

> **Umesh Tips**
>
> AWS free tier includes 50GB data transfer out, 2,000,000 HTTP, and HTTPS requests with Amazon CloudFront.

5.6 Amazon API Gateway

API Gateway is a fully managed service, that makes developers to create, maintain, publish, monitor, and secure APIs at any scale. As we are aware that APIs act as the "front door" for applications to access data, business logic, or functionality from your backend services. It is easy to create RESTFul APIs and WebSocket APIs that enable real-time to two-way communication for applications. The major advantage is it supports serverless and containerized work as well as web applications.

It manages all the tasks involved in handling hundreds of thousands of concurrent API calls, including traffic management, CORS support, and authentication.

Some of the features of API Gateway are as follows:

- **Easy API Creation and Deployment:** API Gateway allows you to create quick and easy custom API for your code running in lambda.
- **API Operation Monitoring:** It gives a dashboard that provides information about calls to the service. API Gateway is integrated with CloudWatch, which helps to

get information about latency and error rates.

- **API Keys for Third-Party Developers:** It helps to create an API key for third-party developers to utilize these APIs.

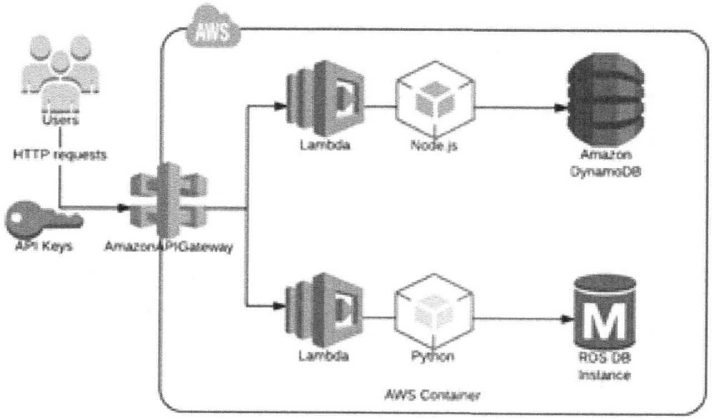

Figure 78

However, API keys can never be considered as a complete security measure as we often store these keys in client applications to call the API. There are two terms when defining a usage plan on AWS API Gateway, and these are throttling and quota. Throttling is about controlling requests per second. By using the Token Bucket Model, the throttling plan can be implemented. At the same time, the quota is defining a number of API requests per specific interval such as day, week, or month.

[8]Cross-origin resource sharing is a mechanism that allows restricted resources on a web page to be requested from another domain outside the domain from which the first resource was served.

5.7 Elastic Load Balancing

It is a load balancer that distributes the load across all the resources for better performance and proper utilization of resources. It is designed in such a way that it can handle the unpredictable load of your application traffic in a single availability zone or across multiple availability zones.

Elastic load balancing offers the following three types of load balancers.

Application Load Balancer

Network Load Balancer

Classic Load Balancer

All three load balancers have the feature of high availability, automatic scaling, and robust security necessary to make your applications fault-tolerant.

Application Load Balancer: This is a layer 7 type of load balancer, it routes traffic to EC2 instances, containers, lambda functions, and IP addresses based on its request. It is ideal for a web-based application that has HTTP or HTTPS traffic, a type of advanced load balancing. The Container-based applications, Microservices, are some of the modern application architectures that are delivered with an advanced level of rounding of the application load balancer.

Network Load Balancer: It operates at the connection level, i.e., layer 4. It routes connections to targets - Amazon EC2 instances, microservices, and containers within Amazon VPC based on IP protocol data. It is ideal for load balancing of both TCP and UDP traffic. A network load balancer is capable of handling millions of requests per second while maintaining ultra-low latencies. It is optimized to handle sudden and volatile traffic patterns while using a single static IP address per availability zone. It is integrated with other popular AWS services such as Auto Scaling, Amazon EC2 Container Service (ECS), Amazon CloudFormation, and AWS Certificate Manager (ACM).

Classic Load Balancer: It provides basic load balancing across multiple Amazon EC2 instances and operates at both the request level and connection level. It is intended for applications that were built within the EC2-Classic network. To use Virtual Private Cloud (VPC), we recommend Application Load Balancer for Layer 7 and Network Load Balancer for Layer 4.

The difference between these load balancer is as follows:

Features of Load Balancer	Application Load Balancer	Network Load Balancer	Classic load balancer
Layer	It works on layer 7	It works on layer 4	It is a tradition-al type of load balancer and it works at layer 7
Service level in AWS	It works on VPC level	It works on VPC level	It works at both VPC and EC2 instance level
Protocols	It allows load balancing at HTTP and HTTPS protocol.	It works at TCP,UDP, and TLS protocol	It works on HTTP/HTTPS, TCP, SSL/TLS protocol
Load bal-ancing to multiple ports on the same instance	Possible	Possible	Possible

Features of Load Balancer	Application Load Balancer	Network Load Balancer	Classic load balancer
Web socket	It is possible to work with WebSocket request	It can handle WebSocket request	Not possible
Lambda Function as target	Possible	Not possible	Not possible
Configurable idle connection timeout	Possible	Not possible	Possible

The following diagram explains the working of the application load balancer.

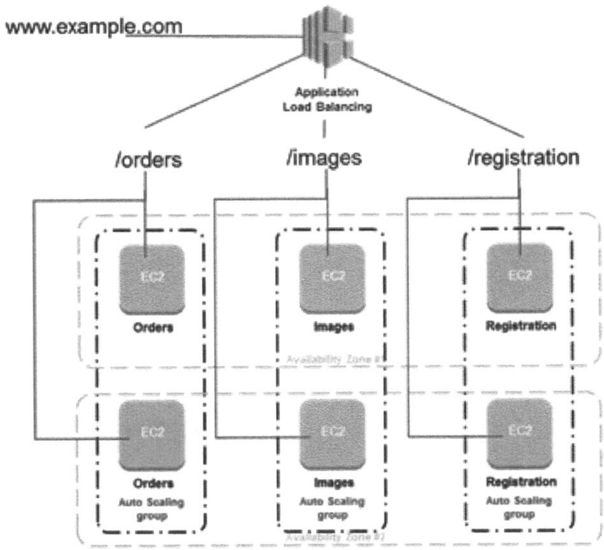

Figure 79

The above figure shows how load-balancing is happing for this particular website traffic.

Practise it, Lets go to next day.

Day 6

3 case studies

Lab - 1

CHAPTER *Six*

File System and Storage in Cloud

CHAPTER POINTS

- **What is the file system in the AWS cloud?**
- **How can these file systems be utilized?**
- **Do the file system needs to connect to the EC2 image?**
- **Can a file system be utilized in isolation?**
- **Can we mount the file system as we use to do with Network File System (NFS)?**

6.1 Introduction to File System and Storage in Cloud

Amazon cloud has a wonderful type of file system. Amazon Web Services (AWS) provides low-cost data storage with both high durability and availability. AWS offers storage choices for backing up information, archiving, and disaster recovery.

Specifically, in storage arena AWS gives three widely used services — Elastic Block Store (EBS), S3, and Elastic File System (EFS) — these file system works differently with each other and offers a respective level of performance, cost, scalability, and availability.

1. **Elastic Block Store (EBS)** – It is a file system that will be available with an EC2 server image. Mostly root partition will be developed using EBS file system
2. **Elastic File System (EFS)** – Mostly it is used for creating other data partitions or drives. It is attached externally to the EC2 server.
3. **S3** – It is a file system that is independent of the EC2 server. It doesn't need an EC2 server attachment to access it. It has the following type of S3 storage classes

- S3 Standard
- S3 Standard-IA
- S3 Intelligent-Tiering
- S3 One Zone-IA
- S3 Glacier

- S3 Glacier Deep Archive

Let's first discuss S3 storage services in the AWS cloud.

Amazon Simple Storage Service (Amazon S3)

Amazon S3 is serverless storage, it does not require an EC2 instance to be attached. You only require isolated S3 storage, hosted on the AWS server and it can be accessed by your application, like in VM and a local server, you need VM to attach storage. In AWS, you can use storage independent of any server.

AWS S3 has countless features such as appending metadata tags to the objects (such as you can name the object, you can tag the purpose of this object or the specific portion of the application that these object will use, makes it easy to locate them), cost efficiencies, enforce security, and it meets compliance requirements. These features can be used to consolidate and manage your data in ways that support specific use cases.

The resource where data is stored is called "Buckets." The single bucket can store up to 5 terabytes of data. S3 has multiple types of storage, basically divided into its cost and availability. You can move data into these buckets of S3 with that you can enforce data access or secure data against unauthorized users. Moreover, you can also run a big data analysis at both the object and bucket level. The fundamental entities of S3 are the objects stored in buckets. Buckets organize the Amazon S3 namespace at the highest level and identify the account responsible for that storage. Amazon S3 buckets are similar to Internet domain names. Objects stored in the buckets have a unique key value and are retrieved using an HTTP URL address. For example, if an object with a key-value /pictures/myhouse.jpg is stored in the AWS-s3-bucket3 bucket, then it is addressable using the URL http://aws-s3-bucket3.s3.amazonaws.com/pictires/myhouse.jpg.

> **Umesh Tips**
>
> S3 Buckets is an entity for regional purposes.

Amazon S3 is designed to deliver 99.999999% durability, it stores millions of file data from many market leaders of the industry. The below figure is representing the case where the S3 bucket is hosting a static website. It is connected to that domain which user can directly access through the AWS cloud.

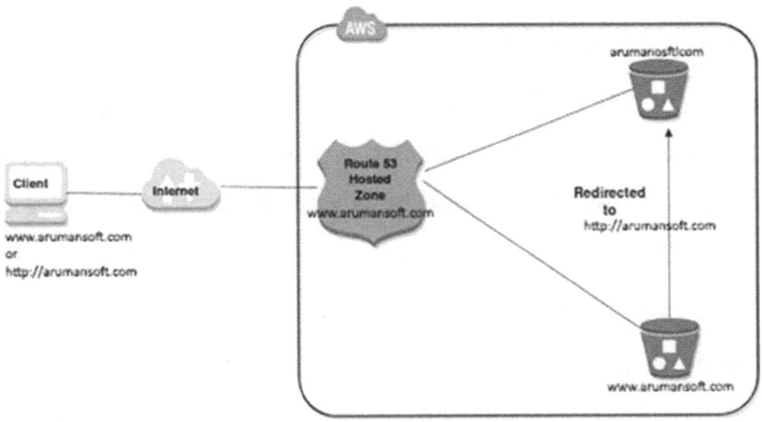

Figure 80

The above image, you can see, is a case where the S3 bucket is hosting a static website. It is mapped to a domain in which end-user can openly access over AWS cloud. Amazon S3 is intended to deliver 99.999999% stability. AWS S3 stores millions of files from many market leaders, they trust its purpose and working as well as durability.

Using Prefixes, all objects stored in S3 buckets can be organized.

You can also append up to 10 key-value pairs called "S3 object tags" to each object. These "S3 object tags" can be created, updated, and deleted throughout an object's lifecycle. To keep a trail of objects and their corresponding tags, buckets, and prefixes, you can use an S3 inventory report. This report lists your kept objects inside an S3 bucket or with an exact prefix and their particular metadata and encryption report. S3 Inventory can be scheduled/configured to automate reports on a daily or a weekly basis.

Features of S3

Reliable Security: After the creation of the S3 bucket, it can be operational only by the identity that has created them (IAM policy grants are the exception).

Each file in this bucket can have separate access permissions. For each bucket, or via IAM(Identity access management), gives full control over how, where, and by whom the data can be accessed. Unauthorized access can be control by NACLs, with these set of rules and permissions.

All-time Availability: It is available up to 99.99%, backed by the Amazon S3 SLA (Service Level Agreement). It is rigorously followed by Amazon.Amazon S3 provides every single user, its service right to use the highly scalable, reliable, fast, low-cost data storage arrangement that Amazon uses to run its international network of websites.

Note S3 Standard is designed for 99.99% availability and Standard – IA is designed for 99.9% availability.

Low cost: Amazon S3 allows you to recompense for the data you use. For infrequent use it is itself a very low price, equivalent to

$0.022 / GB and ~$0.0125 / GB. Moreover, you can also define policies to migrate the data automatically to the infrequent access that further reduces the cost as Amazon Glacier is even cheaper (~$0.004 / GB).

With Amazon S3, you only r recompense for the data you use, which in itself is a very low price equivalent to $0.022 / GB and ~$0.0125 / GB for infrequent access. You can also define policies to migrate the data automatically to infrequent access, which further reduces the cost as Amazon Glacier is even cheaper(~$0.004 / GB).

Ease of Migration: Amazon S3 has numerous cost-effective options for Cloud Data Movement, such as the S3 command-line interface, resync, and glacier command-line interface, and so on. Amazon S3 makes it easy and simple to move a large chunk of data into it or out of it. Moreover, Amazon S3 also provides you the option to import or export data to any physical device or on any network.

With Amazon S3 you get numerous options like S3 command-line interface, resync, and Glacier command-line interface for Cloud Data Movement which is cost-effective. With Amazon S3 it is very easy and simple to move a large chunk of data to Amazon S3 or out of Amazon S3. Amazon S3 also provides you with the option to import or export data to any physical device or on any network.

The Simplicity of Management: Amazon S3 had a user responsive web interface that takes out the typical hard work of sustaining security, optimizing storage, and dealing with the data in the most suitable way. You can outline its lifecycle policy, describe replication rules, and configure the Amazon S3 inventory.

Moreover, to have a better look at your storage it also allows you to configure request metrics and storage class analysis with many filters.

Let us see some case studies to know more benefits of Amazon S3:

Case Study:1

Context:

A website is dedicated to parcel home delivery, where the delivery guy takes the photo and signature of customers accepting the package.

Challenge:

Lots and lot of images getting uploaded by each delivery boy. These images are sent to the vendors. So, the size of storage might be the issue with normal hosting.

Solution:

Amazon S3 has unlimited storage. You can pay for as much memory you utilized. Moreover, you can also have an automated archiving system for low-cost storage. After a certain time, these will be deleted as per your SLA or configuration.

Suppose you have a website that is for parcel home delivery, where the delivery guy takes a photo customer accepting the package and signature of the customer. Lots and a lot of images are getting upload from each of the delivery boys. Those need to be sent to the vendor who has booked these deliveries. So the size of storage might be an issue with normal hosting.

But with Amazon S3, it is unlimited. You need to pay for as much memory you utilized. You can have an automated archiving system for low-cost storage. After a certain time, these will be deleted as per your SLA or configuration.

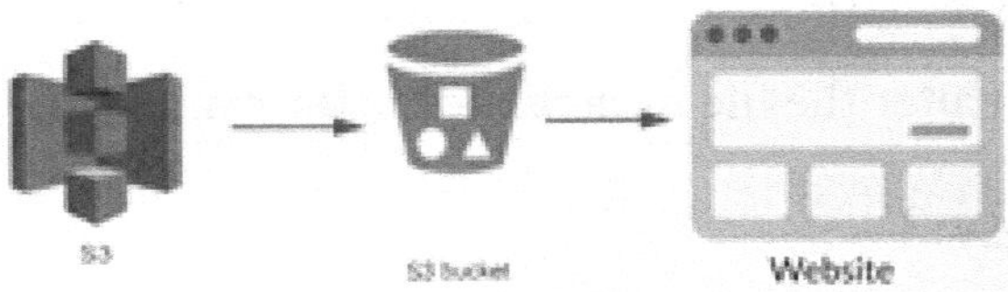

Figure 81

Case Study:2

Context:

A social media mobile application is collecting photos uploaded by a user daily.

Challenge:

Some of the photos which were uploaded a few days back may not have much importance. Those photos may not be required on the user dashboard/wall daily; they may be accessed once in a couple of months.

Solution:

These types of photos can be moved to other categories of S3 storage, which is cost-effective. This doesn't end any intervention by the user. Automatically this movement can happen after the life cycle policy is implemented.

For example, a social media mobile app is used for uploading thousands of user pics. Certain upload which was done before seven days back do not have that importance, and those are not needed on the user dashboard/wall. Those will be accessed once in a couple of months. These kinds of photos can be moved to other categories of S3 storage, which is cost-effective. This doesn't end any intervention by the user; automatically, this movement will happen after the life cycle policy is implemented.

Case Study:3

Context:

Database backup daily incremental

Challenge:

Low-cost storage needed with instant access

Solution:

On business infrastructure setup, SQL server incremental backup is being taken daily and full backup weekly. It is being written to the S3 bucket. As per policy, on the very next working day, the backup copy is moved to S3 IA, which is a less costly file system.

After a particular period, these backup files are moved to S3 Glacier. This is being configured in the lifecycle of these files.

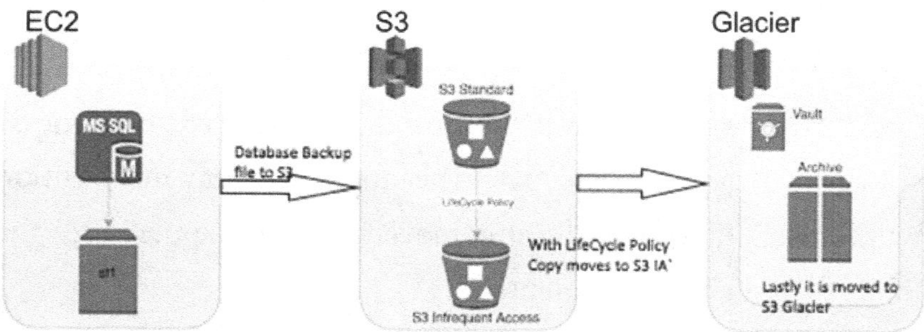

Figure 82

Types of S3 File System

S3 Infrequent Access (Amazon S3 IA): S3 IA is designed for data that is less frequently accessed but requires rapid access when required. S3 Standard-IA offers high durability, high throughput, and low latency of S3 Standard, with a low per GB storage price and per GB retrieval fee. This combination of low cost and high performance makes S3 Standard-IA ideal for long-term storage, backups, and as a data store for disaster recovery.

S3 One Zoned-IA: S3 One Zoned-IA is designed for data that is accessed less frequently but requires rapid access when needed. Unlike other storage classes, which stores data in a minimum of three availability zones (data centers), S3 One Zone-IA stores data in a single AZ. This results in storing data in S3 One Zone-IA costs 20% less than storing it in S3 Standard-IA. It's a good choice, for example, for storing secondary backup copies of in-premises data or easily re-creatable data.

S3 Reduced Redundancy Storage: Reduced Redundancy Storage (RRS) is an Amazon S3 storage option that enables customers to store non-critical data. Moreover, it also stores reproducible data at lower levels of redundancy than the Amazon S3's standard storage. It provides a highly available solution for distributing or sharing content that is durably stored elsewhere. For storing thumbnails, transcoded media, or other processed data can be easily reproduced. The RRS option stores objects on multiple devices across multiple facilities, providing 400 times the durability of a typical disk drive but it does not replicate objects as many times as standard Amazon S3 storage.

It is designed to provide 99.99% of both durability and availability of objects over a given year

The durability level corresponds to an average annual expected loss of 0.01% of objects. Moreover, it is designed to sustain the loss of data in a single facility.

Topic	Standard S3	S3 – Infrequent Access	S3 – Reduced Redundancy Storage
Durability	99.999999999%	99.999999999%	99.99%
Availability	99.99%	99.9%	99.99%
Concurrent facility fault tolerance	2	2	1
SSL Support	Yes	Yes	Yes
First-byte latency	Millisecond	Millisecond	Millisecond
Lifecycle management policies	Yes	Yes	Yes

Amazon Glacier: Amazon Glacier is a secure, durable, and very low-cost storage service for data archiving. Customers can store data for as small as $0.004 per gigabyte per month. To keep costs low yet suitable for varying retrieval needs, Amazon Glacier provides different options for access to archives, from a few minutes to several hours.

AWS offers two types of Glacier storage solutions, namely Glacier and Deep Glacier

- **Glacier:** As we have discussed above Glacier, is storage used for archiving data. It is much more economical than the S3 standard but its retrieval time is high.
- **Deep Glacier:** All objects stored in the S3 Glacier Deep Archive storage class are replicated and stored across at least three geographically-dispersed Availability Zones, protected by 99.999999999% durability, and can be restored within 12 hours or less. Moreover, S3 Glacier Deep Archive also offers a bulk retrieval option, where you can retrieve petabytes of data within 48 hours. Along with seven different storage class options, today, Amazon S3 also provides the broadest array of cost-optimization options available in the cloud. S3 Glacier Deep Archive expands our data archiving offerings, enabling you to select the optimal storage class based on storage, and retrieval costs, and retrieval times. Choose S3 Glacier for archived data if you want retrieval options in minutes.

To retrieve data stored in S3 Glacier Deep Archive, you can initiate a “Restore” request using the Amazon S3 APIs or the Amazon S3 Management Console. The Restore creates a temporary copy of your data in the S3 RRS storage class while leaving the archived data intact in S3 Glacier Deep Archive. You can specify the amount of time in days for which the temporary copy is stored in S3. Then you can access your temporary copy from S3 through an Amazon S3 GET request on the archived object.

The easiest way to store data in S3 Glacier Deep Archive is to use the S3 PUT API to upload data directly. You can also upload data to S3 Glacier Deep Archive over the Internet or using AWS Direct Connect and the AWS Management Console, AWS Storage Gateway, AWS Command Line Interface, or the AWS Software

Development Kit. S3 Glacier Deep Archive is integrated with Tape Gateway, a cloud-based virtual tape library feature of AWS Storage Gateway. Along with this capability, you can now manage your in-premises tape-based backups and reduce monthly storage costs by choosing to archive your new virtual tapes in either the S3 Glacier or S3 Glacier Deep Archive storage classes.

Umesh Tips

Cross Account permission is required to be done by using Policy, not by just IAM permissions.

Topic	Standard S3	Glacier
Performance	Access to Amazon S3 from within Amazon EC2 in the same region is fast.	It is slow as a job typically takes 3 to 5 hours to complete the data pulling job.
Cost	Higher than Glacier.	As little as $0.01 per gigabyte per month.
Payment Pattern	Pay only for what you use. There is no minimum fee.	Pay only for what you use. There is no minimum fee.
Cost dependency	Three pricing components: storage (per GB per month), data transfer in or out (per GB per month), and requests (per thousand requests per month).	You can retrieve up to 5% of your average monthly storage (pro-rated daily) for free each month

Topic	Standard S3	Glacier
Capacity	They were designed to offer a very high level of scalability and elasticity automatically.	A single archive is limited to 4 TBs,but there is no limit to the total amount of data you can store in the service.
Number of files	Supports a virtually unlimited number of files in any bucket.	Whether you are storing petabytes or gigabytes, Amazon Glacier automatically scales your storage up or down as needed.

Umesh Tips

S3 Buckets "Name" should be unique for overall amazon (not just regain or AZ).

Lab 1-Procedure to Create S3 File System

Let us try to create the first S3 file system in our account and let us see the options of the S3 file system. Once this Lab is completed, you will be able to do the following procedures:

Upon completion of this Lab, you will be able to:

1. Create an S3 bucket
2. Create a folder within an S3 bucket
3. Upload content to S3
4. Change permissions to allow public access to content

5. Set metadata on an S3 bucket
6. Delete an S3 bucket and its contents

Follow the procedure, as shown below:

1. Get authenticated, go to the Amazon account.
2. On the menu, under the storage section, S3 is displayed.
3. Click Create bucket.

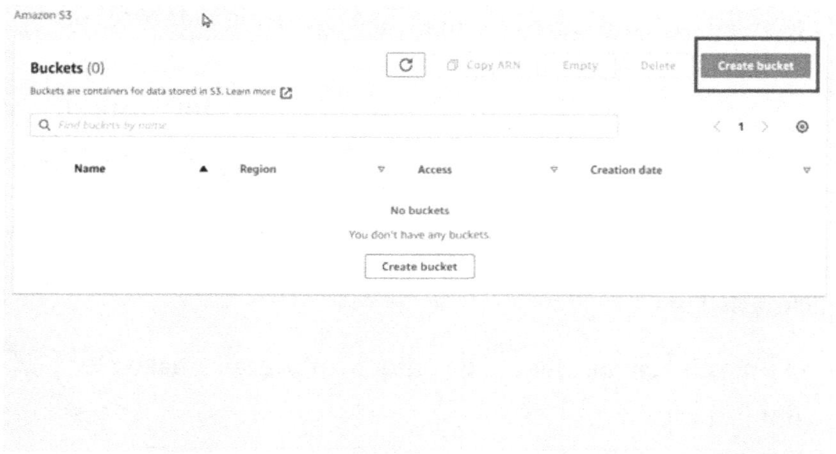

Figure 83

This will create a bucket

Amazon Elastic File System (Amazon EFS)

We have one of the directories which are shared across the network, usually called a shared directory. You may have seen a couple of RDBMS system like DB2 has shared directory across multiple servers. You can create a certain directory that is mapped to a couple of servers, i.e. Network file system. We have seen NFS mount points across UNIX base server or windows has directory shared from server, mapped as the drive to desktops. These are network file systems.

Similarly, Amazon offers EFS, it is called an elastic file system. It is the same as of network file system. It is a simple, scalable, and fully managed elastic network file system (EFS). It can be utilized for cloud services as well as in-premises resources.

It is built to scale up to Petabyte, without disturbing the application where it is connected. It will grow and shrink as you add or remove the file from this location, eliminating the need for capacity management to accommodate the growth.

It offers two types of storage system:

1. Standard EFS storage (EFS)
2. Infrequent access storage (EFS IA)

How to utilize this infrequent access storage (EFS IA)? It is not a very technical task, you just have to enable lifecycle management on your file system. Those files which are not accessed according to your lifecycle policy will be transparently moved to EFS IA. This will result in good saving, as it is seen that 80% of files are not accessed very frequently on such type of file system. Only 20% of files are accessed more frequently, resulting in storage cost as low as 0.08$ /GB-Month*.

EFS is best used for supporting a broad spectrum of use cases from workloads. Like Workloads, that require high throughput to the one-threaded kid of workloads. Use cases like shift and lift enterprise applications, you can connect EFS to the in-premises server, you can put application data on this, which can be mapped to the EC2 server. Moreover, you can also do container storage, large database backups, entertainment workflows where video and images of large size are stored, media, application development, content management, web serving, and Big Data analytics.

Let us see the benefit of EFS:

- **Compliance and Security:** EFS helps you to securely access your files by using your security Infrastructure. You can get control access to your EFS file system with Amazon VPC, AWS IAM. Moreover, you can secure data by encrypting data at rest. AmazonEFS get in touch with many compliance and eligibility needs to connect with regulatory needs.
- **Best Price:** Pay only for what you use. There is no requirement of provision storing in advance, and no minimum fee is required. You can simply move files that are not accessed for 30 days, for a cost-optimized storage class, by decreasing storage costs up to 85 %.
- **Completely Managed:** EFS is a totally managed service for offering shared file system storage for Linux workloads. It offers an easy interface to design and configure file systems. This will configure the file system very fast and manage file storage infrastructure for you. Moreover, it terminates the complexity of moving and maintaining.
- **Shared File Storage:** EFS offers secure access for hundreds of connections, for example, EC2 and in-premises servers. They continuously access shared Amazon EFS by implementing, hierarchical directory design by NFSV4 (Network File System Protocol). EC2 Instances access your file system on many AZs and regions where in-premises-server access using AWS

VPN or AWS Direct connect.

- **Measurable Performance:** Amazon EFS, designed to offer IOPS (Input/Output Operations Per Second) and less latency required for Linux workloads. Throughput and IOPS measure as a file system grows and that can burst to high throughput levels for short periods with unpredictable requirements and performance needs. For most demanding workloads, Amazon EFS supports 10GB/second and 500,000 IOPS.
- **Elasticity:** Amazon EFS instantly and automatically measures your system life and storage capacity. You can add or remove files without interrupting your applications and offering the storage that you need. When you need it, you can simply design your file system and you can start adding files with no provision storage in advance.
- **Container Storage:** Containers are known as an integral part of designing microservices. They need fast to provision and simple to portable and offer process isolation. Containers require access to original data when they start every time. They have to take advantage of a secured and shared file system.
- **Entertainment:** Sound designing, broadcast processing, studio production, and video editing them often work on shared storage to control large file system. Amazon EFS offers a strong data consistency sample with a large throughput.
- **Application Development and Testing:** Amazon EFS

offers your development environments in the same storage repository. It gives you the ability to distribute your code and another file in an organized way.

You can create one or more EFS file systems within an AWS Region. Each file system is accessed by EC2 instances via mount targets, which are created per Availability Zone. You can create one mount target per Availability Zone. In the VPC you can create using Amazon Virtual Private Cloud. Traffic flow between Amazon EFS and EC2 instances is controlled by using the security groups associated with the EC2 instance and the EFS mount targets. Access to EFS file system objects (files and directories) is controlled by using standard Unix-style read/write/execute permissions based on user and group IDs.

Amazon Elastic Block Store (Amazon EBS)

We have seen that our Laptop, desktop, or server is having a certain GB/TB of storage attached to it, which is known as server disk/storage. This type of disk can be attached to anyone's server. This disk belongs to a particular computing machine. Similarly, the cloud has storage called an Elastic block store (EBS).

These are storage which is having a file system as per the operating system of the EC2 server. These are always connected to one instance of the EC2 server, it can not be connected to multiple servers i.e. EC2 instance at a time.

EBS also provides the ability to create point-in-time snapshots of volumes, which are stored in Amazon S3. These snapshots can be used as the starting point for new EBS volumes and to protect data for long-term durability. The same snapshot can be used to instantiate as many volumes as you want. These snapshots can be copied across AWS regions, making it easier to leverage multiple AWS regions for geographical expansion, data center migration, and disaster recovery. Sizes for EBS volumes range from 1 GB to 16 TB, depending on the volume type, and are allocated in 1 GB increments.

Amazon EBS is meant for data that changes relatively frequently and needs to persist beyond the life of EC2 instance. Amazon EBS is well-suited for use as the primary storage for a database or file system, or any application or instance (operating system) that requires direct access to raw block-level storage. Amazon EBS provides a range of options that allows you to optimize storage performance and cost for your workload. These options are divided into two major categories: solid-state drive (SSD)-backed storage for transactional workloads such as databases and boot volumes (performance depends primarily on IOPS) and hard disk drive (HDD)-backed storage for throughput-intensive workloads such as big data, data warehouse, and log processing (performance depends primarily on MB/s).

Topic	SSD Backed Provisioned IOPs (io1)	SSD-Backed General Purpose (gp2)	HDD-Backed Throughput Optimized (st1)	HDD-Backed Cold (sc1)
Use Cases	I/O-intensive NoSQL and relational databases	Boot volumes, low-latency interactive apps, dev & test	Big data, data ware house, log processing	Colder data requiring fewer scans per day
Max IOPS** per Volume	20,000	10,000	500	250

Topic	SSD Backed Provisioned IOPs (io1)	SSD-Backed General Purpose (gp2)	HDD-Backed Throughput Optimized (st1)	HDD-Backed Cold (sc1)
Volume Size	4 GiB – 16 TiB	1GiB – 16 TiB	500 GiB – 16 TiB	500 GiB – 16 TiB
Max Throughut per Volume	320 MiB/s	160 MiB/s	500 MiB/s	250 MiB/s
Max IOPS per Instance	65k	65k	65k	65k
Max Through put per Instance	1250 MB /s	1250 MB /s	1250 MB /s	1250 MB /s
Dominant Performance Attribute	IOPS	IOPS	IOPS	IOPS

AWS Site Comparison

There is no separate data API for instance store volumes. Just like EBS volumes, instance store volumes present a block-device interface to the EC2 instance. To the EC2 instance, an instance store volume appears just like a local disk drive. To write to and read data from instance store volumes, you use the native file system I/O interfaces of your chosen operating system.

Amazon EC2 Instance Storage

In general, EC2 local instance store volumes are ideal for the temporary storage of information that is continually changing, such as buffers, caches, scratch data, and other temporary content.

Moreover, it is also ideal for data that is replicated across a fleet of instances, such as a load-balanced pool of web servers. EC2 instance storage is well-suited for this purpose. It consists of the virtual machine's boot device (for instance store AMIs only), plus one or more additional volumes that are dedicated to the EC2 instance (for both Amazon EBS AMIs and instance store AMIs). This storage can only be used from a single EC2 instance during that instance's lifetime. Note that, unlike EBS volumes, instance store volumes cannot be detached or attached to another instance.

For high I/O and high storage, use EC2 instance storage targeted to these use cases. High I/O instances (the i2 family) provide instance store volumes backed by SSD and are ideally suited for many high-performance database workloads. Example applications include NoSQL databases like Cassandra and MongoDB, clustered databases, and online transaction processing (OLTP) systems. High storage instances (the d2 family) support much higher storage density per EC2 instance and are ideally suited for applications that benefit from high sequential I/O performance across very large datasets. Example applications include data warehouses, Hadoop/MapReduce storage nodes, and parallel file systems.

Limitations of Instance Store Volumes

Instance store volumes are complicated and you need to get to know their limitations before you decide to use it as a storage option. Below are some of the limitations of instance store volumes:

- To deliver very high random I/O performance, instance store volumes only run on solid-state drives (SSD).

- It only supports C3, G2, HI1, I2, I3, M3, R3, and X1 instance families.
- Data in the instance store can be lost if the underlying disk drive fails or if the instance stops, or if the instance terminates.
- Instance store devices have only root volume, which can not be extended. You can have storage space of 350GB on instance store volumes. If OS supports, you can manage 350GB of space by partitioning root volume.
- It is not possible to resize instance-backed root volumes on the fly. You will need to create an AMI and then launch a new instance from that AMI and giving it a bigger instance store.
- Taking a snapshot or create AMI of an instance to back up the instance storage. It is not as straightforward as taking a snapshot of EBS volume.
- When a new volume is attached, instance store volumes attached to certain instances will suffer a first-write penalty which might affect I/O of the storage. The only way this will not happen is if they are already initialized before they are in-use.
- Some special instance types use NVMe or SATA-based solid-state drives (SSD) to deliver very high random I/O performance.
- A few instance types such as c1.medium and m1.small include a 900 MB instance store swap volume, which may not be automatically enabled at boot time.

- Instance store volumes are included as part of the instance's hourly cost.

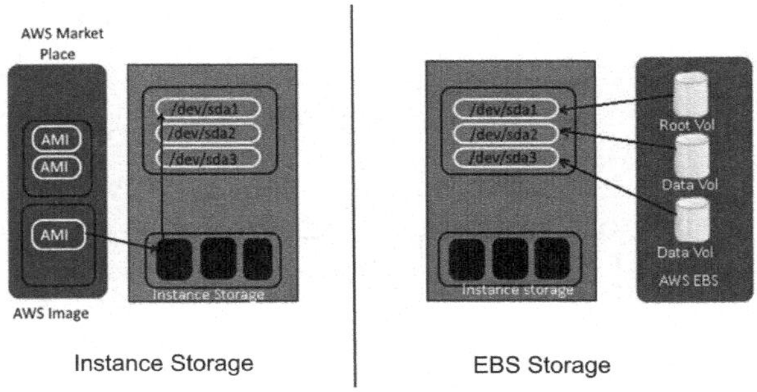

Figure 84

Difference between Instance storage and EBS (Elastic Block Storage) are as follows:

Sr. No.	Instance storage	EBS
1	Instance store volumes access torage from disks that are physically attached to the host computer.	EBS volume is a network-attached drive.
2	An instance store is ephemeral storage that provides temporary block-level storage for your instance.	Volume persists independently from the running life of an instance. After an EBS volume is attached to an instance, you can use it like any other physical hard drive.
3	It is fast as it is attached to the host server.	It is a network block drive attached to a particular instance.

Sr. No.	Instance storage	EBS
4	Instance store backed instances can be of a maximum 10GiB volume size.	It can be attached in a terabyte, as much as 16 TiB per volume.
5	Data of instance storage is lost in the following scenario: • Underlying disk failed • Instance stop • Instance termination	Data of EBS storage is NOT lost in the following scenario: • Reboot on the Instance • Stopping an EBS-backed instance • Termination of the Instance

AWS Storage Gateway

Storage Gateway is a service in AWS that connects an in-premises software appliance with cloud-based storage. This service provides secure integration between an organization's in-premises IT environment and AWS storage infrastructure. Storage Gateway service allows you to securely store the data in the AWS cloud for scalable and cost-effective storage.

Storage Gateway is a virtual appliance that is installed in a hypervisor running in a data center used to replicate the information to the AWS particularly S3. Amazon Storage Gateway's virtual appliance is available for download as a virtual machine (VM) image which you can install on a host in your data center.

Storage Gateway supports either Vmware EXI or Microsoft Hyper-V. Once you have installed the storage gateway, link it with your AWS account through the activation process, and then you can use the AWS Management Console to create the storage gateway option.

There are three types of storage gateway:

1. File Gateway (NFS)
2. Volume Gateway (iSCSI)
3. Tape Gateway (VTL)

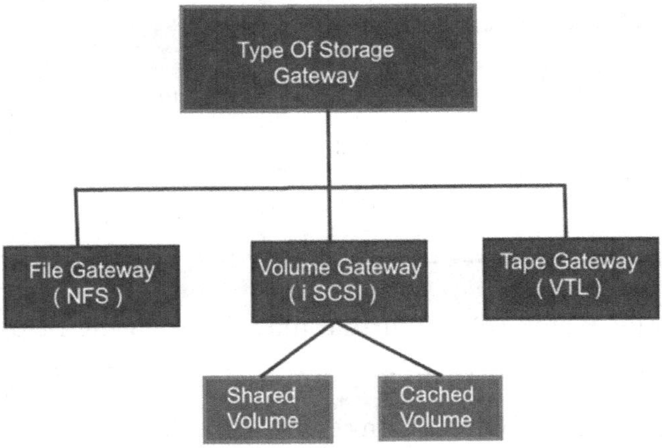

Figure 85

File Gateway

File Gateway uses the technique Network File System (NFS). It is used to store the flat files in S3 such as word files, pdf files, pictures, videos, etc. It is used to store the files to S3 directly. Files are stored as objects in S3 buckets, and they are accessed through an NFS mount point. The ownership, permissions, and timestamps are durably stored in S3 in the user metadata of the object associated with the file.

Once the objects are transferred to the S3, they can be used as the native S3 objects, and bucket policies such as versioning, lifecycle management, and cross-region replication can be directly applied to the objects stored in your bucket.

Figure 86

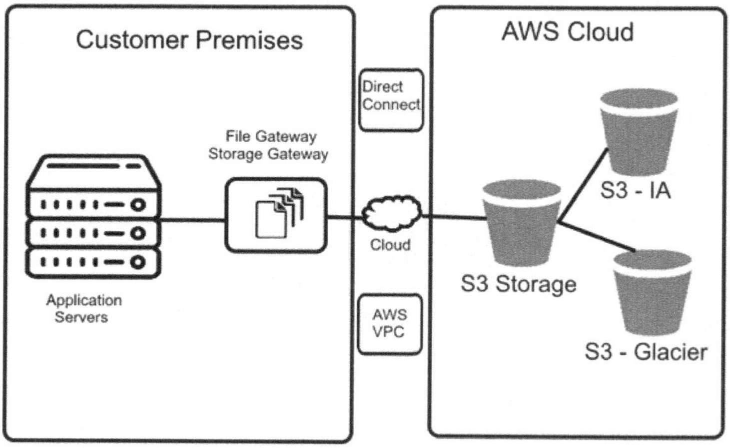

SG (Storage Gateway) is a virtual machine running in-premises. Storage Gateway is mainly connected to AWS through the Internet. It can use Direct Connect which is a

direct connection line between the Data Center and AWS.

SG can also use an Amazon VPC (Virtual Private Cloud) to connect a storage gateway to AWS. VPC is a virtual data center that represents that the application server and storage gateway do not need to be in-premises. In Amazon VPC, the storage gateway sits inside the VPC, and then the storage gateway sends the information to S3.

Volume Gateway

Volume Gateway is an interface that presents your applications with disk volumes using the Iscsi block protocol. The iSCSI block protocol is block-based storage that can store an operating system, applications and also can run the SQL Server database. Data written to the hard disk can be asynchronously backed up as point-in-time snapshots in your hard disks and stored in the cloud as EBS (Elastic Block Store) snapshots. EBS is a virtual hard disk that is attached to the EC2 instance. In short, we can say that the volume gateway takes the virtual hard disks that you back them up to the AWS. Snapshots are incremental backups so that the changes made in the last snapshot are backed up. All snapshot storage is also compressed to minimize your storage charges.

Stored Volume

Stored Volume is a way of storing the entire copy of the data locally and asynchronously backing up the data to AWS. Stored volumes provide low-latency access to the entire datasets of your on-premise applications and offsite backups. You can create a stored volume that can be a virtual storage volume which is mounted as iSCSI devices to your on-premise application services such as data services, web services.

Data written to your stored volume is stored on your local storage hardware, and this data is asynchronously backed up to the Amazon Simple Storage Services in the form of Amazon Elastic Block Store snapshots. The size of the stored volume is 1GB - 16 TB.

Cached Volume

Cached volume is a way of storing the most recently accessed data on-site, and the rest of the data is stored in AWS. Cached Volume allows you to use the Amazon Simple Storage Service as your primary data storage while keeping a copy of the recently accessed data locally in your storage gateway. Cached Volume minimizes the need to scale your in-premises storage infrastructure while still providing low-latency access to their frequently accessed data.

Cached Gateway stores the data that you write to the volume and retains only recently read data in in-premises storage gateway. The size of the cached volume is 1GB-32 TB.

Tape Gateway

Tape Gateway is mainly used for taking backups. It uses a Tape Gateway Library interface. Tape Gateway offers a durable, cost-effective solution to archive your data in the AWS cloud. The Virtual Tape Library (VTL) interface provides a tape-based backup application infrastructure to store data on virtual tape cartridges that you create on your tape Gateway. It is supported by NetBackup, Backup Exec, Veeam, and so on. Instead of using physical tape, they are using virtual tape, and these virtual tapes are further stored in Amazon S3.

To summarize the storage gateway:

- **File Gateway:** It is used for object-based storage in which all the flat files such as word files, pdf files, and so on are stored directly on S3.
- **Volume Gateway:** It is used for block-based storage, and it is using an iSCSI protocol.
- **Stored Volume:** It is a volume gateway used to store the entire dataset on-site and backed up to S3.
- **Cached Volume:** It is a volume gateway used to store the entire dataset in a cloud (Amazon S3) and only the most frequently accessed data is kept on site.
- **Tape Gateway:** It is used for backup and uses popular

backup applications such as NetBackup, Backup Exec, Veeam, and so on.

AWS Snowball

It is a petabyte-scale data transport solution provided by amazon. It uses a secure application to transfer large data into the AWS cloud. Moreover, you can get large data out of the cloud using snowball. It effectively addresses the problem of high network costs while transferring large data. It also addresses time improvement for large of amount data with security into consideration.

Some of the key features of AWS Snowball are as follows:

- **Fast Data Transfer:** Snowball Edge devices feature high-speed network connections, supporting 10 Gbps to 100 Gbps links with RJ45, SFP+ and QSFP+ copper, and optical interfaces. All encryption is performed on the device itself, helping enable a higher data throughput rate and shorter data transfer times.
- **Secure Erasure:** Once the data transfer job has been processed and verified, AWS performs a software erasure of the Snowball Edge device that follows the National Institute of Standards and Technology (NIST) guidelines for media sanitization.

Some of the benefits of Snowball are as follows:

- **Speed:** It is the biggest benefit of using AWS Snowball. It could take months to transfer 50TB of data even with high-speed internet connections, and transferring that much data over the internet is often not feasible. Using Snowball, you can transfer 50TB onto a Snowball in less than a day (depending on your local environment) and have the data on AWS within a week, including shipping times.

- **Simple and Compatible:** Using AWS Snowball is simple and compatible with your network and applications. The user can connect Snowball through industry-standard network interfaces such as 10Gb Ethernet via RJ45, copper SFP+ and optical SFP+ adapters, and storage protocols like HDFS, the S3 API, and the S3 CLI.

Lets practice about file system. Next day we are doing to look into services which are serverless.

♦ ♦

Day 7
Lab 3
1 case study

CHAPTER *Seven*

Serverless Services

CHAPTER POINTS

- **What is a serverless service?**
- **How does Lambda work in AWS?**
- **How is AWS Cloud Watch used for monitoring?**
- **How is the database serverless?**
- **Is data transfer between the Application server and CloudFront is chargeable?**

7.1 Serverless Services

Serverless computing architecture eliminates infrastructure management tasks such as patching, provisioning, operating system maintenance as well as scaling, and capacity planning. This mode allows you to build and run an application without preparing the infrastructure. Serverless service gives the developer a chance to focus on the core product and to innovate applications and solutions. It results in faster development of applications. It enables simplified operational management and scaling of applications and operational cost reduction.

AWS provides serverless services in many areas such as computing, messaging, integration, security, monitoring with a database, and analytics. One by one, let us look into it.

Sr. No.	Area of Computing	Service Name
1	Compute	• AWS Lambda • AWS Fargate
2	Messaging	• Amazon SQS • Amazon SNS
3	Integration	• Amazon API Gateway • AWS Step Function
4	Security	• Amazon Cognito • AWS key management

Sr. No.	Area of Computing	Service Name
5	Monitoring	• Amazon CloudWatch • Amazon Quicksight
6	Database	• Amazon Dynamo DB • Amazon Aurora
7	Analytics	• Amazon Kinesis • Amazon Athena

1. **AWS Lambda:** Lambda is the FaaS (Function as a Solution) solution from AWS where you can run code for any type of application or backend service. For example, certain data upload to be done in the database by using files uploaded on S3, you can evoke a function on file upload event, which will pull data from the file and insert it into the database.

Lambda can help you to execute code as a function triggered by various event sources, for example, HTTP requests on AWS API Gateway, file updates on S3, or metric alarms in AWS CloudWatch. It runs the code on a fully-managed, high-available infrastructure and performs all administrative tasks of the compute resources, including server and system maintenance, capacity provisioning and automatic scaling, code monitoring, and logging. You have to pay only for the compute time that your application actually consumes. Lambda can be combined with many other AWS services and is used in many scenarios, such as authorizing an HTTP request by validating a JSON web token, real-time filtering, and transforming streaming data, processing data in S3, managing database handling, and many more.

Cross-device development is a huge concern when it comes to application development. Facilitating this comes at a high cost and manual task, which hinders the efficiency of development teams. However, with AWS Lambda, you can solve and automate this problem by developing a multi-platform media and content delivery pipeline.

For example, whenever a user requests an image which is not available in the Amazon S3 bucket, the user's browser follows the redirect and request the image resize through AWS API Gateway. This triggers the Lambda function, which fetches the original image from the S3 bucket, resizes it, and uploads it back along with the corresponding requested key.

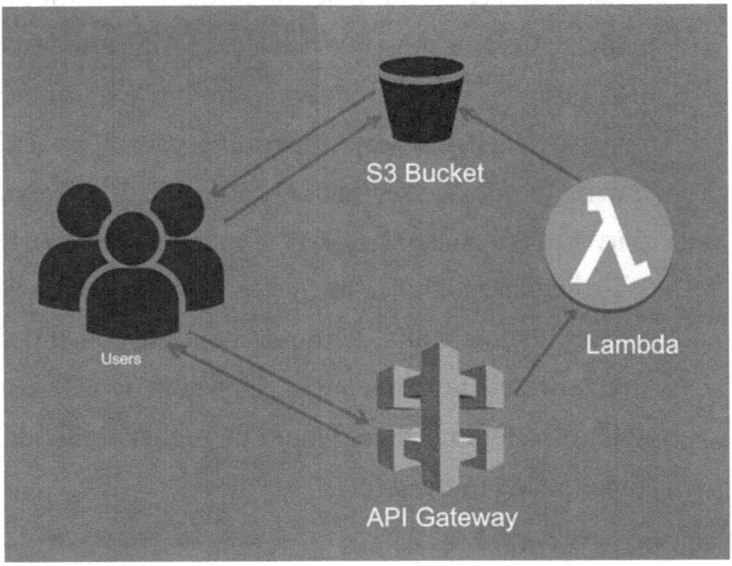

Figure 87

The best example is Netflix, with its 70 billion hours of content

in a quarter to nearly 60 million customers, uses AWS Lambda examples of media transform to facilitate their media files in more than 50 formats. They are also leveraging it to build a self-sufficient automated infrastructure to replace inefficient processes to reduce the error rates and valuable time.

The major areas where AWS Lambda helps are when you're redesigning your website or app. You don't need to resize your entire image archive. Transformation on the go gives you high agility. Due to on-demand image resizing, you are not required to store your archive in every possible format. Moreover, you can also delete the expired and older images. In Lambda, each request is initiated if the required image is not available. This means that each request is not affected in any way by the previous failover.

2. **AWS Fargate:** It is the containerization service of AWS, where you can run Docker containers without any management of servers or clusters. Amazon describes it as a way to "Run containers without managing servers or clusters." It is a way of running your apps without having to manage servers or scaling clusters. Fargate is part of the Amazons Elastic Container Service (ECS). It is the perfect choice for developers who want to run apps with low traffic without spending too much on overpowered EC2 instances. However, it will also be able to scale up if there would be higher traffic during some points in the day.

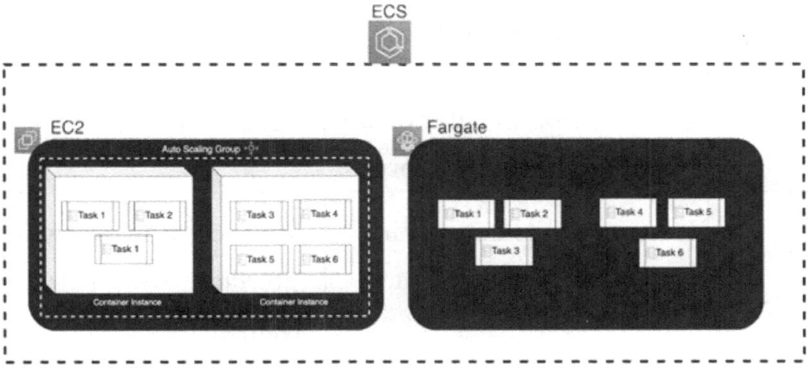

Figure 88

I actually believe that Containers as a Service (CaaS) is the real PaaS that developers have been waiting for years. It allows developers to deploy their containers directly in the cloud without having to worry about everything in between. I find this point critical for a lot of tech startups. In fact, sometimes one of your competitive advantages is the use of a state-of-the-art technology that you have participated in developing or the smart re-use of another one in a totally new and revolutionary context.

Serverless deployment allows you to focus on writing great code. No provisioning, easy scaling.

Sr. No.	EC2 container Instance	Fargate
1	Pricing for this type of cluster is as many EC2 instances work for that particular time.	Pricing for this is per running task by this cluster.
2	You have to maintain these instances. So very high operation efforts are required	Since it is a container as service, very low maintenance is required for this cluster

Sr. No.	EC2 container Instance	Fargate
4	EFS and EBS integration are possible with some efforts.	Not possible
5	It has multiple networking options available with it.	An elastic network interface per task is available.

3. **Amazon SQS:** Queues are a powerful way of combining software architectures. They allow for asynchronous communication between different systems and are especially useful when the throughput of the systems is unequal. Amazon offers their version of queues with Amazon SQS (Simple Queue Service).

Let us see some examples if one of the systems have something like:

- **System Message Producer** – Produces messages periodically in huge bursts.
- **System Message Consumer** – Consumes messages constantly, at a slower pace.

In this architecture, a queue would allow System A to produce messages as fast as it can, and System B to slowly digest the messages at its own pace.

Queues have played an integral role in software architecture for decades, along with core technology concepts like APIs (Application Programming Interfaces) and ETL/ELT (Extract, Load Transform). As the recent trend is inclined towards Microservices, queues have become more important than ever.

Amazon offers a queueing service with the name of Simple Queue Service (SQS). SQS is a fully managed message queuing service that enables you to decouple and scale microservices, distributed systems, and serverless applications. SQS eliminates the complexity and overhead associated with managing and operating message-oriented middleware and empowers developers to focus on differentiating work. Using SQS, you can send, store, and receive messages between software components at any volume, without losing messages or requiring other services to be available. You can get started with SQS in minutes by using the AWS console, Command Line Interface, or SDK of your choice, and three simple commands.

SQS offers two types of message queues. Standard queues and FIFO (First In First Out) queues. The standard queues offer maximum throughput, best-effort ordering, and at-least-once delivery, whereas FIFO queues are designed to guarantee that messages are processed exactly once, in the exact order that they are sent.

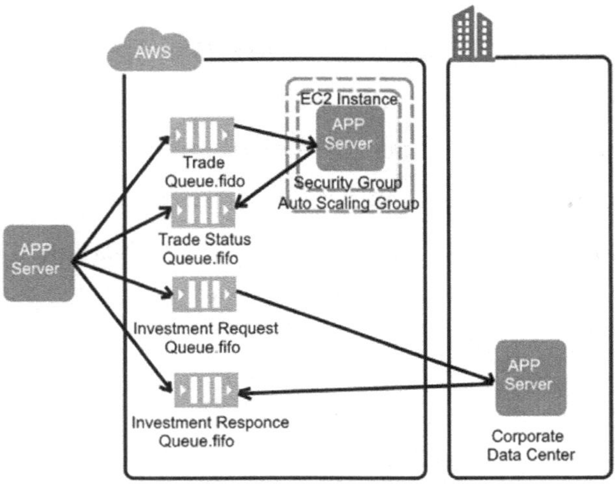

Figure 89

4. **Amazon Simple Notification Service:** SNS is a simple notification service, it can trigger, by event, a Lambda function, EC2 instance using SQS, Email, or Smart Phone Notification.

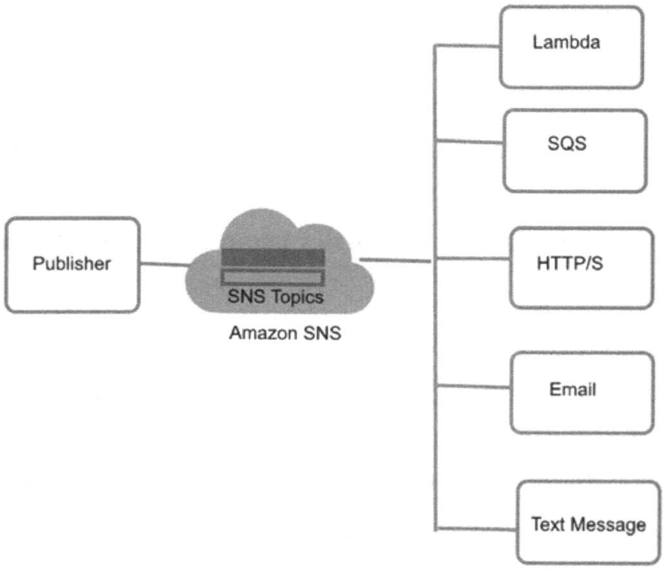

Figure 90

It is a web service that makes it easy to set up, operate, and send a notification from the cloud. It provides developers with a highly scalable, cost-effective, and flexible capability to publish messages from an application and sends them to other applications. It is a way of sending messages. If you are using AutoScaling, it triggers an SNS service that will email you that "your EC2 instance is growing".

SNS can also send messages to devices by sending push notifications to Apple, Google, Fire OS, and Windows devices, as well as Android devices in China with Baidu Cloud Push. Besides sending the push notifications to the mobile devices, Amazon

SNS sends the notifications through SMS or email to an Amazon Simple Queue Service (SQS) or an HTTP endpoint.

SNS notifications can also trigger the Lambda function. When a message is published to an SNS topic that has a Lambda function associated with it, the Lambda function is invoked with the payload of the message. Therefore, we can say that the Lambda function is invoked with a message payload as an input parameter and manipulate the information in the message and then sends the message to other SNS topics or other AWS services. Amazon SNS allows you to group multiple recipients using topics where the topic is a logical access point that sends identical copies of the same message to the subscribed recipients.

Amazon SNS supports multiple types of endpoints. For example, you can group IOS, Android, and SMS recipients. Once you publish the message to the topic, SNS delivers the formatted copies of your message to the subscribers. To prevent the loss of data, all messages published to SNS are stored redundantly across multiple availability zones.

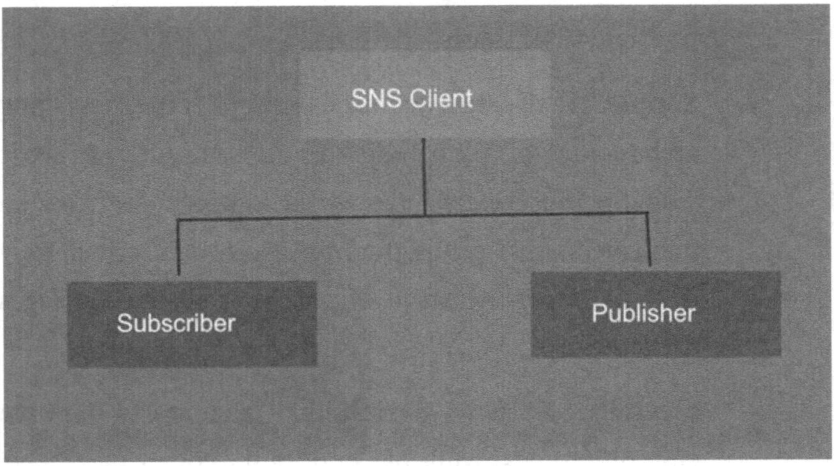

Figure 91

SNS is a web service that manages to send messages to the subscribing endpoint. There are two clients of SNS:

1. Subscribers
2. Publishers

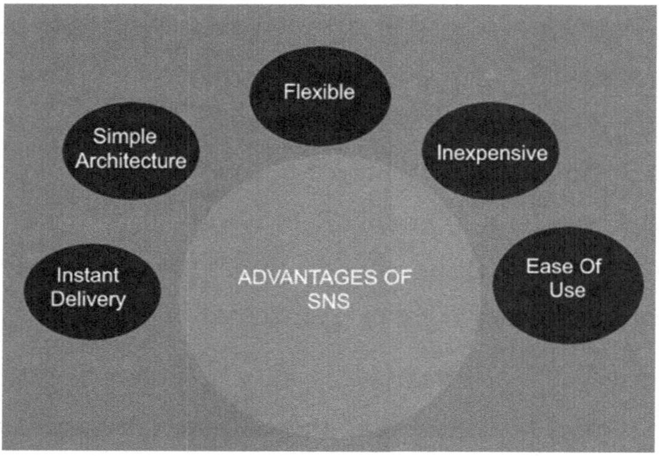

Figure 92

Advantages of SNS service are as follows:

- **Instance Delivery:** SNS is pushed once you publish the message in a topic, and the message is delivered to multiple subscribers.
- **Simple Architect:** SNS is used to simplify the messaging architecture by offloading the message filtering logic from the subscribers and message routing logic from the publishers. SNS sends the message to subscriber-only of their interest, instead of receiving all the messages from the topic.
- **Flexible:** SNS is so flexible that it supports multiple endpoint types. Multiple endpoint types can receive the message over multiple transport protocols such as

email, SMS, Lambda, Amazon SQS, HTTP, and so on.

- **Inexpensive:** SNS service is quite inexpensive as it is based on the pay-as-you-go model, i.e., you need to pay only when you are using the resources with no up-front costs.
- **Ease of Use:** SNS service is very simple to use as the web-based AWS Management Console offers the simplicity of the point-and-click interface.

The difference between SNS and SQS are as follows:

No.	SNS	SQS
1	SNS stands for Simple Notification Service.	SQS stands for Simple Queue Service.
2	SNS is a push-based delivery. As in notification is pushed to multiple clients.	SQS is pulled based delivery. User application or user has to pull messages from the queue.
3	SNS service is pushed to multiple receivers.	As clients pull the message, so no multiple clients for this service are required
4	SNS pushing pushes the messages to the subscribers immediately.	SQS polling introduces some latency in message delivery.

5. **Amazon API Gateway:** Amazon API Gateway is a managed service that allows developers to define the HTTP endpoints of a REST API or a WebSocket API. It connects those endpoints with the corresponding

backend business logic. It also handles authentication, access control, monitoring, and tracing of API requests. Many serverless applications use Amazon API Gateway, which conveniently replaces the API servers with a managed serverless solution.

API Gateway sits between the backend services of your API and your API's users. It handles the HTTP requests to your API endpoints and routing them to the correct backends. It provides a set of tools that help you to manage your API definitions and the mappings between endpoints and their respective backend services. Moreover, it can generate API references from your definitions and make them available to your users as API documentation.

API Gateway integrates with many other AWS services such as AWS Lambda, AWS SNS, AWS IAM, and Cognito Identity Pools. These integrations allow for fully managed authentication and authorization layers, as well as detailed metrics and tracing for API requests.

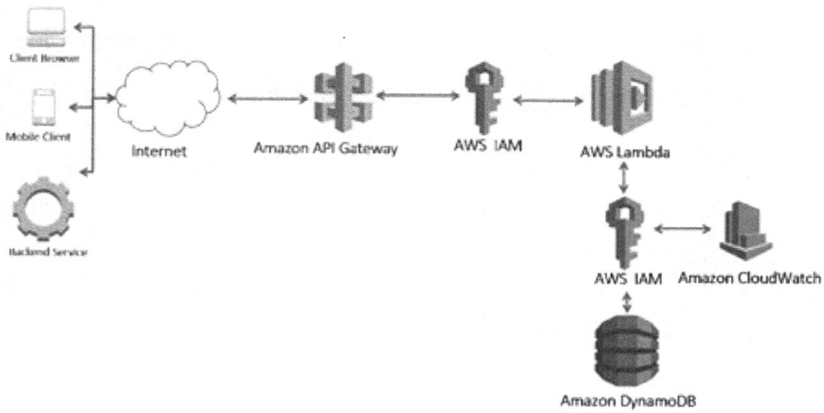

Figure 93

Many AWS services support integration with Amazon API Gateway. HTTP API responses are generated to run the Lambda function. Publish SNS notification when an HTTP API endpoint is accessed. Amazon Cognito provides authentication and authorization for your HTTP APIs.

6. **AWS Step Function:** Orchestrating a series of individual serverless applications, managing retries, and debugging failures can be challenging. As your distributed applications become more complex, the complexity of managing them also grows. Step Functions automatically manages error handling, retry logic, and state. It has its built-in operational controls, by which it manages sequencing, removing a significant operational burden from your team.

AWS Step Functions is a serverless function orchestrator that makes it easy to sequence AWS Lambda functions and multiple AWS services into business-critical applications. Through its visual interface, you can create and run a series of checkpointed and event-driven workflows that maintain the application state. The output of one step acts as input into the next. Each step in your application executes in order and as expected, is based on your defined business logic.

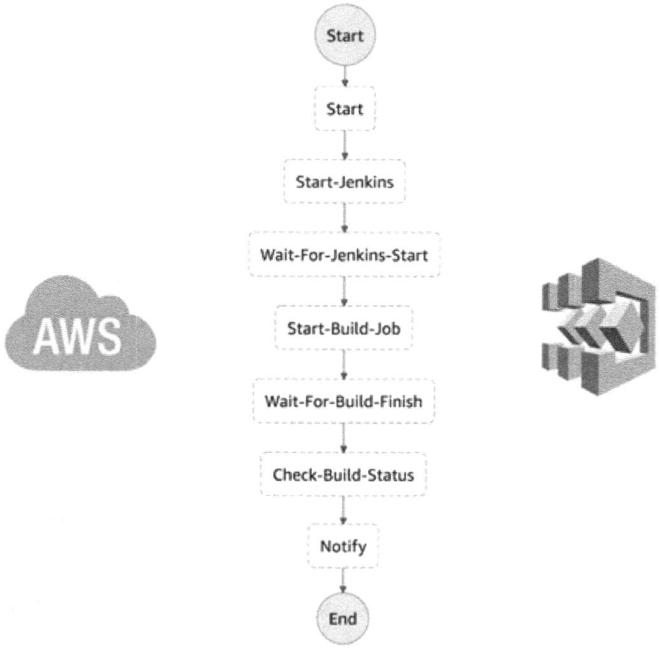

Figure 94

7. **Amazon Cognito:** Amazon Cognito is a fully-managed, scalable, and cost-effective sign-up/sign-in service, provides user authentication, authorization, and management for both web and mobile applications. The two main components of Amazon Cognito are user pools and identity pools.

    - **User Pools:** It is a user directory, that provides sign-up and sign-in services, based on its own or an external identity provider that implements the SAML, OAuth2, or OpenID connect protocol, such as Facebook or Google. You can use a customizable web UI for the user sign-in, which can be integrated into your existing webpage.

- **Identity** Pool: In this, your authorized user or anonymous guest can exchange user pool tokens for temporary AWS credentials to access AWS resources. You can grant your users or groups fine-grained access to your resources or AWS services, based on IAM role policies. Moreover, Cognito, has advanced security features, such as e-mail, phone verification, and multi-factor authentication.

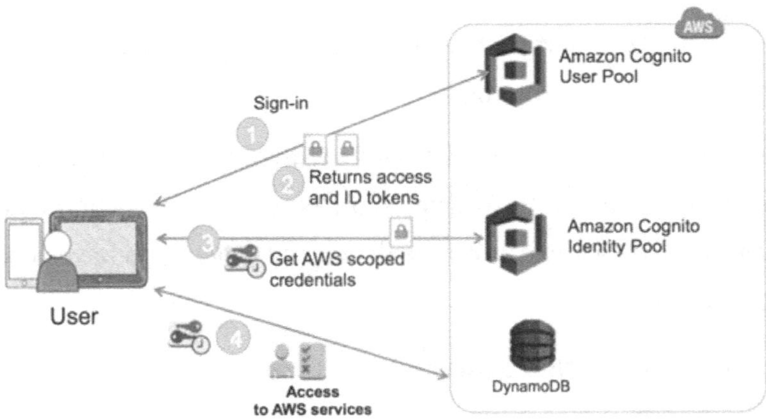

Figure 95

8. **KEY Management System (KMS):** As per Amazon, AWS Key Management Service (AWS KMS) is a managed service that makes it easy for you to create and control the encryption keys used to encrypt your data. The master keys that you create in AWS KMS are protected by FIPS 140-2 validated cryptographic modules.

The primary resources in AWS KMS are Customer Master Keys (CMKs). You can use a CMK to encrypt and decrypt up to 4 KB

(4096 bytes) of data. Typically, you use CMKs to generate, encrypt, and decrypt the data keys that you use outside of AWS KMS to encrypt your data. This strategy is known as envelope encryption.

- **Encryption Process:**

    1. Generate a data key using the GenerateDataKey operation of AWS KMS.

The operation returns a plaintext copy of the data key and a copy of the encrypted data key by using the Customer Master Key (CMK).

2. Encrypt the data with the plain data key and destroy the key.

We can store this encrypted key along with our encrypted message. The message can not be decrypted unless you can decrypt the data key and the data key can not be decrypted unless you have access to the master key.

- **Decryption Process:**

    1. To get the plain data key, decrypt the encrypted key using our master key.
    2. Decrypt the data with the plain data key.

Decrypt the encrypted key using our master key to get the plain data key.

Decrypt the data with the plain data key.

Types of AWS KMS

There are three types of AWS KMS, they are as follows:

1. Customer Managed CMK

2. AWS Managed CMK
3. AWS Owned CMK

- **Customer Managed CMK:** CMKs that you create, own, and manage. You have full control over these CMKs.
- **AWS Managed CMK**: CMKs that are created, managed, and used on your behalf by an AWS service that is integrated with AWS KMS. Some AWS services support only an AWS managed CMK.
- **AWS Owned CMK**: CMKs that an AWS service owns and manages for use in multiple AWS accounts. You do not need to create or manage the AWS owned CMKs.

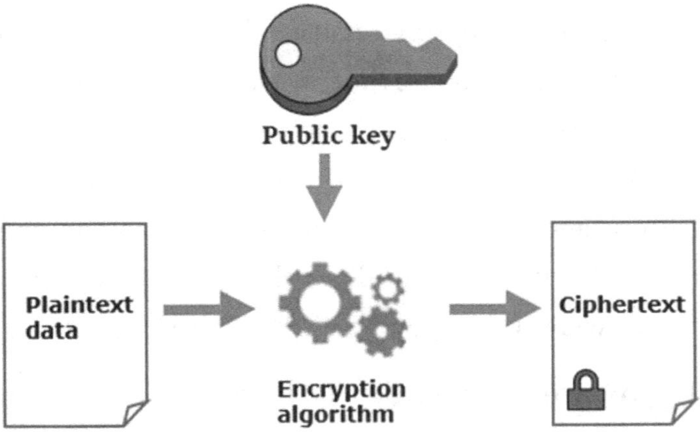

Figure 96

9. **Amazon CloudWatch**: This is a monitoring system present in Amazon. We will look in detail in the chapter that describes Monitoring Tools.

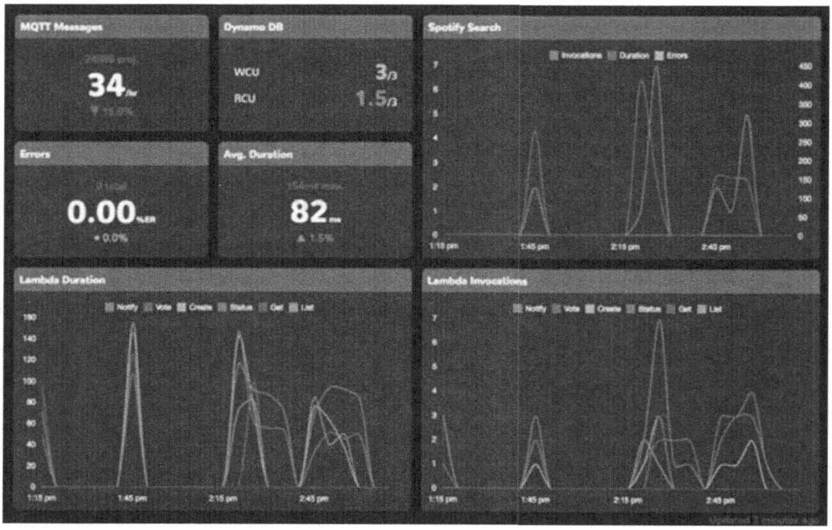

Figure 97

CloudWatch collects data from a resource like EC2, RDBMS, Load balancer, and other services, data like network performance, load balancer target response time, availability of service like that. Amazon CloudWatch enables you to collect, access, and correlate this data on a single platform from across all your AWS resources, applications, and services that run on AWS and in-premises servers. It helps you to break down data silos so you can easily gain system-wide visibility and quickly resolve issues.

10. **Amazon Quicksight**: To have the right information at your fingertips is the key to make sound business decisions. Apart from this, your ability to interpret that information and the speed at which you can access it are equally essential. That's where Amazon QuickSight plays an important role.

QuickSight claims to be "a fast, cloud-powered business intelligence service that makes it easy to deliver insights to everyone in your organization." The platform does this with stunning visuals and interactive dashboards that present real-time, machine learning (ML) insights to your company's decision-makers. Amazon QuickSight is a business intelligence tool under the umbrella of the Amazon Web Services (AWS) platform. Since its release, QuickSight is best known for stunning visualizations, interactive dashboards, and accurate machine learning insights.

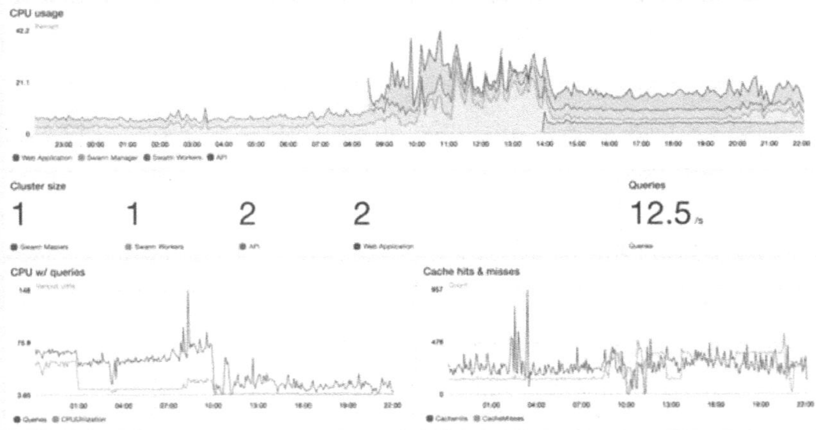

Figure 98

Standard Edition Pricing:

The costs for the Standard Edition (which doesn't include machine learning (ML) insights) is as follows:

which doesn't include machine learning (ML) insights:

- **Authors (Standard Edition)**: The charge is $9 per author per month for an annual subscription and $12 per user per month for a month-to-month subscription. This comes with 10 GB of SPICE per author with the opportunity to purchase more SPICE capacity at $0.25 per GB.

Enterprise Edition Pricing:

The costs for the Enterprise Edition, includes machine learning insights)is as follows:

- **Readers:** The charge is $0.30 per 30 minutes of use per user, for reading privileges only, with a max charge of $5 per month per user.
- **Authors:** The charge is $18 per author per month for an annual subscription or $24 per user per month for a month-to-month subscription. This includes 10 GB of space capacity and authors can purchase additional SPICE capacity for $0.38 per GB.

These are more affordable than competing solutions, but costs can add up. Fortunately, Amazon offers the following "Reader Pricing Scenarios" for the Enterprise Edition to help.

11. **Amazon Dynamo DB:** We have a detailed chapter for the database in this book. We will study more about it in that chapter.
12. **Amazon Kinesis:** As the name suggests, kinesis is a movement or motion that makes it easy to collect, process, and analyze real-time, streaming data. Amazon Kinesis propositions key capabilities to cost-effective practice streaming data at any scale, along with the flexibility to choose the tools that best suit the requirements of your application. Kinesis is proficient in handling hundreds of terabytes per hour from great volumes of streaming data from sources such as operational logs, commercial transactions, and social

media feeds. Agreeing to Amazon, Kinesis plugs a gap missing by Hadoop and former technologies that progress data in batches but that don't empower real-time operative decisions about continuously streaming data. That proficiency, in turn, shortens the process of inscription apps that rely on statistics that must be administered in real-time.

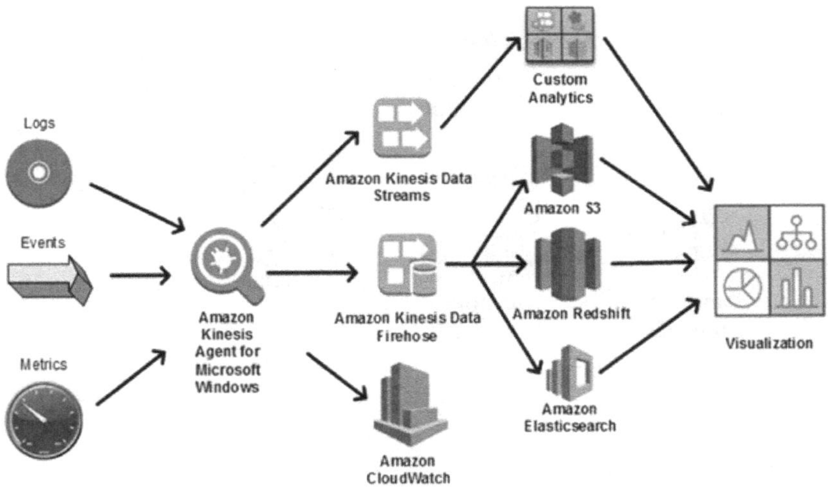

Figure 99

13. **Amazon Athena**: It is an analytical tool and serverless interactive query service. It makes it easy to analyze data present in Amazon S3, using Standard Query Language (SQL). Athena is cool to use. Just point to your records in Amazon S3, describe the schema, and start inquiring using standard SQL. Most results are conveyed within seconds. Using Athena, there is no need for difficult ETL businesses to formulate your data for exploration. This makes it easy for anybody with SQL skills to speedily analyze extensive datasets.

Athena is out-of-the-box cohesive with AWS Glue Data Catalog, countenancing you to create a unified metadata repository across several services, crawl data sources to determine schemas, and inhabit your Catalog with new and altered table and partition descriptions, and maintain schema versioning.

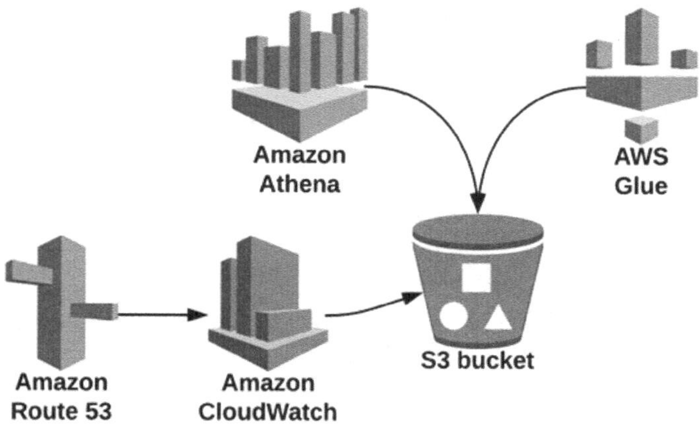

Figure 100

Advantage of Athena:

- **Start Querying Instantly**: It is serverless with no ETL, it serves as ETL for the cloud. You can rapidly request your data without having to set up and cope with any servers or data warehouses. Just plug into your data in Amazon S3, describe the schema, and jump querying via the built-in query corrector/editor. Amazon Athena lets you beat into your data entirely in S3 without the necessity to set up complex processes to extract, transform, and load the data (ETL).
- **Pay Per Query**: It does not need you to set up an EC2 server or Dataware house to query the data. No setup

is needed as infrastructure is concerned. You just need to put data into an S3 bucket and start querying it. So the payment is per query base, no additional costing or maintenance is needed.

- **Open, Powerful, and Standard:** Amazon Athena uses Presto with ANSI SQL support and works with a variety of standard data formats, including CSV, JSON, ORC, Avro, and Parquet. Athena is ideal for quick, ad-hoc querying. Moreover, it can also handle complex analysis, including large joins, window functions, and arrays.
- **Lightning Fast in Work**: Through Amazon Athena, you don't have to concern about having adequate compute assets to get a fast, interactive query presentation. Amazon Athena robotically accomplishes queries in parallel, so the utmost results come back in seconds.

7.2 Introduction to AWS Cloud Front

Amazon CloudFront is a content delivery network (CDN) provided by Amazon Web Services. By using a CDN, companies can accelerate the delivery of files to users over the Internet while also reducing the load on their infrastructure. CloudFront is AWS's own CDN solution that integrates with other AWS products, so it is convenient for companies already running on AWS.

CloudFront acts as a distributed cache for your files, with cache locations around the world. It fetches your files from their source location ("origin" in CloudFront terms) and places the copies of the files in different edge locations across America, Europe, Asia, Africa, and Oceania. In doing this, CloudFront speeds up the access to your files for your end-users.

The below case study shows how does CloudFront is beneficial:

Case Study: 1

Context:

Your data origin is located in Brazil and one of your customers is in Japan would like to access this data. Without CloudFront (or a similar solution), this customer would need to send a request to the other side of the world, transferring the files from a very distant location.

Challenge:

This will result in a request that is slow to arrive at the destination as well as a slow file download. It will make your customers wait long to get data and it could result in a poor customer experience.

Outcome:

- The files are periodically fetched by the CloudFront system from the location in Brazil and placed onto a set of servers around the world, including one in Japan.
- When a user in Japan goes to download the files, the request will now be served by a nearby server with lower latency, a higher download speed, and a better customer experience.

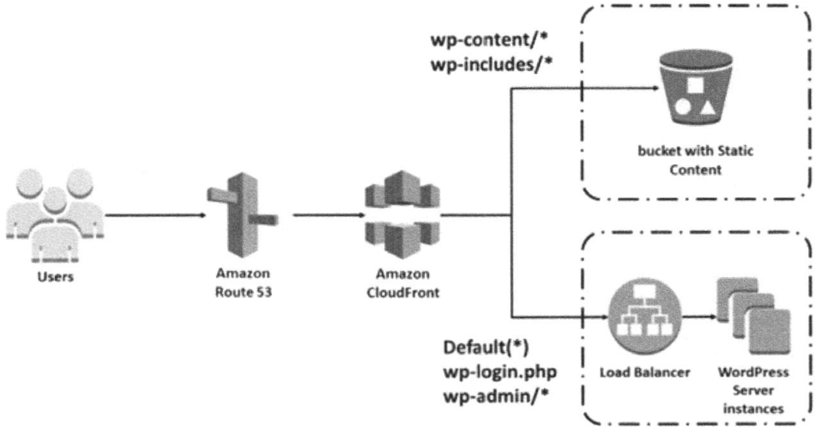

Figure 101

Compute provide a platform/environment to deploy your code. It provides you an environment where you can execute the deployed code.

Since this is very vast subject, we have tried to introduce to these services. We are going to be have in detail explanation in other book.

Lets go to next day, where we will see monitoring tools in detail.

♦ ♦

Day 8
Lab - 1

CHAPTER *Eight*

Monitoring Tools

CHAPTER POINTS

- **What is Cloud Watch?**
- **What is Cloud trail?**
- **How can we set up monitoring using cloud watch?**

8.1 Introduction to Monitoring Tools

When you create the infrastructure and you any customer-facing application,

these applications need to run 24 x 7. Since every application involves a couple of resources to hundreds of resources. It became very difficult to monitor each and every parameter of those resources to see that performance of the application is not degrading. It also became very teddies to monitor logs of every resource. So, to monitor those logs and activities, we use monitoring tools. AWS has its monitoring tools.

Cloud monitoring is a wide-ranging category that comprises observing web and cloud applications, infrastructure, networks, platform, application, and micro-services. Monitoring is critical to make sure that all the amenities which you are consuming on the cloud are running effortlessly and professionally.

Amazon provides two distinct monitoring tools. They are as follows:

1. AWS CloudWatch
2. AWS CloudTrail

Cloud Watch: Amazon CloudWatch is the module of Amazon Web Services that offers real-time checking of AWS assets and customer applications running on Amazon set-up. CloudWatch accumulates monitoring and operational statistics in the arrangement of logs, metrics, and events and visualizes it using programmed dashboards. This can get you an integrated view of your AWS resources, applications, and services that run in AWS and in-premises.

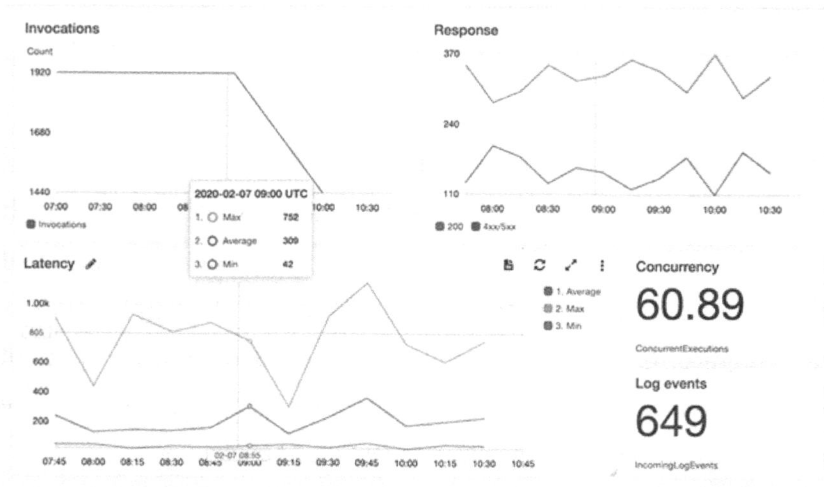

Figure 102

CloudWatch enables robust monitoring of resources such as:

- Virtual instances hosted in Amazon EC2
- Databases located in Amazon RDS
- Data stored in Amazon S3
- Elastic Load Balancer
- Auto-Scaling Groups
- Other Resources

Cloud Watch displays, stocks, and offers access to system and application log documents. It offers a catalog of custom reports that you can use to scrutinize trends and observer system performance. Arrange for various alert capabilities, including rules and triggers high resolutions alarms, and sends notifications. Gathers and delivers a real-time demonstration of operational data in the form of key metrics like CPU utilization, disk storage and so on.

Customers can access admittance CloudWatch utilities over an API, command-line tools, one of the AWS SDK (software development kits), or the AWS Management Console. The CloudWatch edge offers up-to-date statistics that can be seen in graph presentation. Customers can establish notifications (called "alarms") to be propelled when something being supervised surpasses a quantified threshold. The app can also sense and shut down idle or underused EC2 instances.

Certain concepts are essential to know for more understanding of cloutWatch.

Metrics: A metrics represents a time-ordered set of data points that are published to CloudWatch. You can relate a metric to a variable that is being monitored where data points to the value of that variable over time. Metrics are uniquely defined by a name, a namespace, and zero or more dimensions. Each data point has a time-stamp.

Dimensions: A dimension is a name/value pair that uniquely identifies a metric. Dimensions can be considered as categories of characteristics that describe a metric. The reason behind this is dimensions are unique identifiers for a metric; whenever you add a unique name/value pair to one of your metrics, you are creating a new variation of that metric.

Statistics: The statistics are metric data aggregations over specified periods. Aggregations are made by using the namespace, metric name, dimensions within the period you specify. Few available statistics are maximum, minimum, sum, average, and sample count.

Alarm: An alarm can be used to automatically initiate actions on your behalf. It watches a single metric over a specified period and performs one or more specified actions. The action is simply a notification that is sent to the Amazon SNS topic.

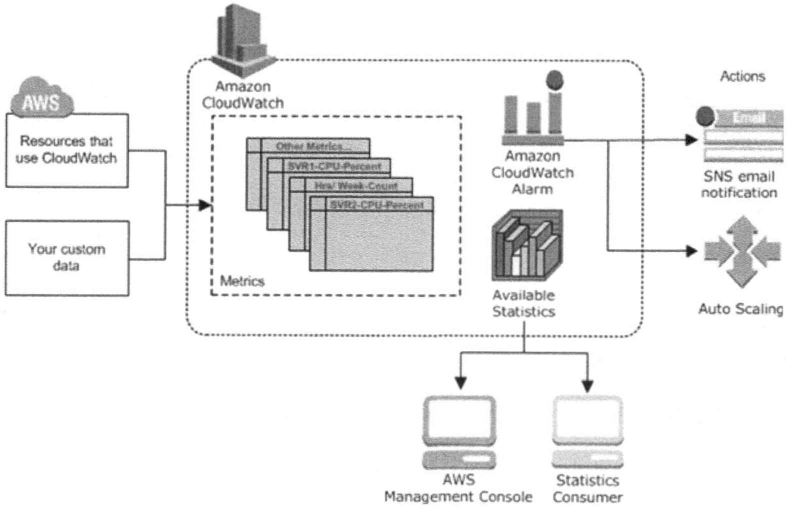

Figure 103

CloudTrail: CloudTrail is an API log observing web service presented by AWS. It allows AWS regulars to record API calls and sends these log collections to Amazon S3 buckets for storing. This facility offers details of API action such as the identity of the API caller, the interval of the API call, the source IP address of the API caller, the applications made, and response essentials are returned by the AWS service. Also, it apprehensions a few non-API proceedings (AWS service events and AWS console sign-in events).

CloudTrail can also be constituted to publish a notification for each log file that is conveyed, consenting customers to take action upon log file delivery.

Lab 1-Procedure to enable CloudTrail

1. Login to the AWS console
2. Go to AWS Services → Management Tools → CloudTrail.

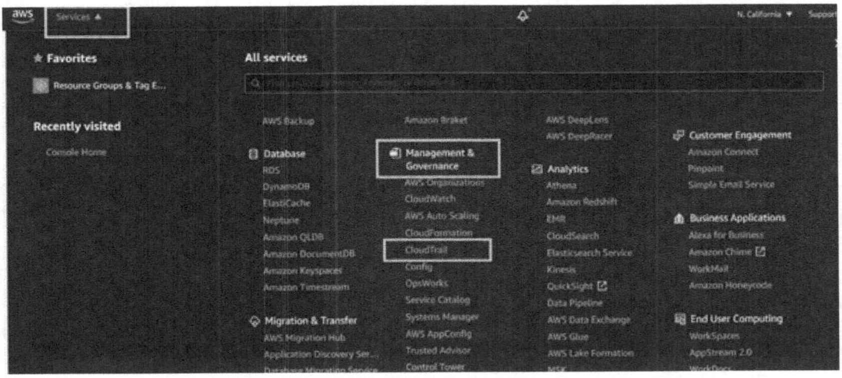

Figure 104

3. Click Add new trail.

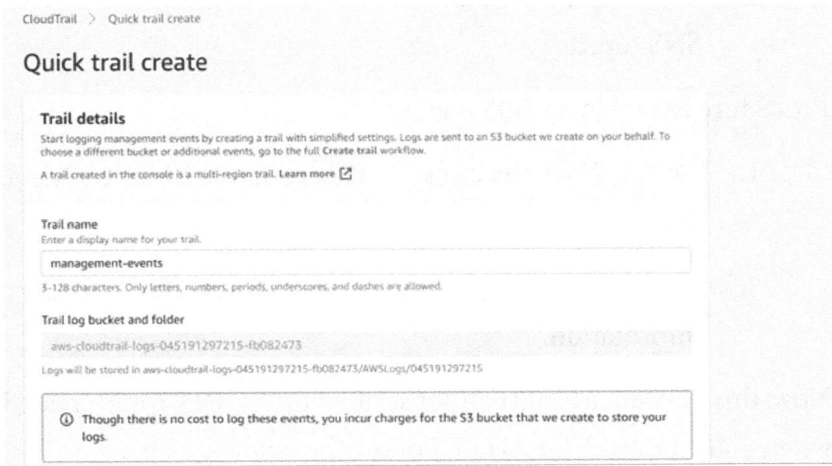

Figure 105

4. Click **Advanced** and fill in the missing information.

Configure an SNS topic:

1. Create an SNS topic.

Refer to the below image for the correct settings.

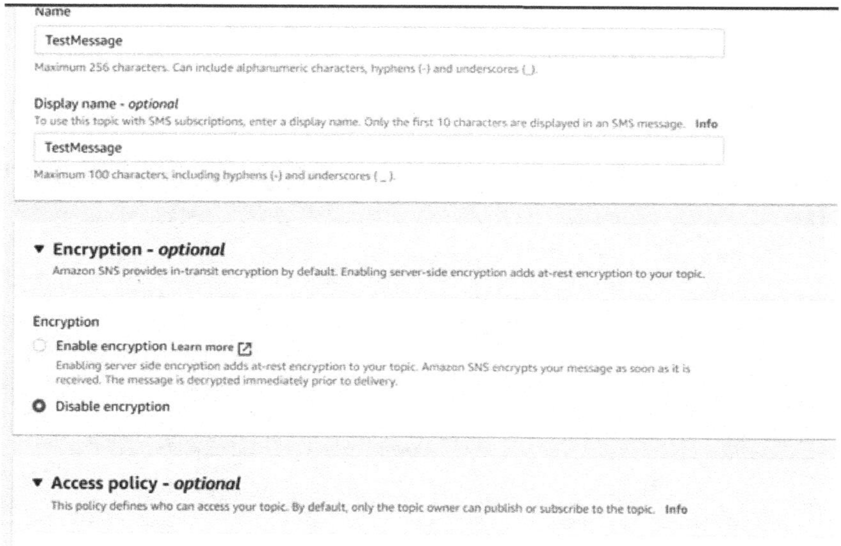

Figure 106

2. Create an SQS queue and subscribe to the above-created SNS topic.

Procedure to create an SQS queue:

1. Go to AWS Services → Messaging → Simple Queue Service (SQS).
2. Click Create New Queue and fill in the necessary information.

Now, this SQS queue must be subscribed to the SNS Topic created when you enabled CloudTrail. Follow the below-given steps.

1. Select the SQS queue created.
2. From the Queue Action drop-down menu, select Subscribe Queue to SNS Topic.

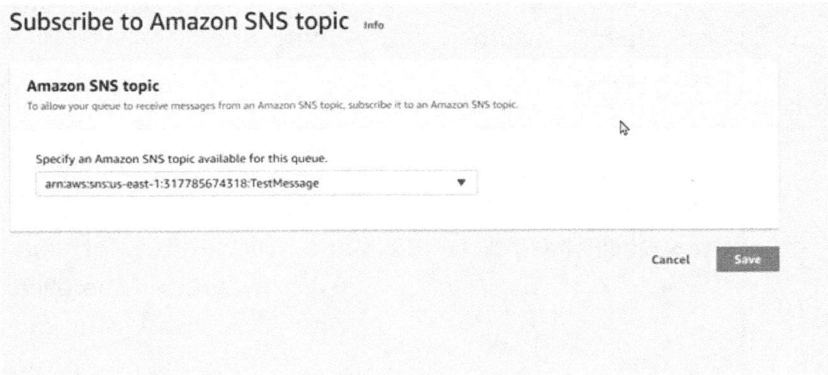

Figure 107

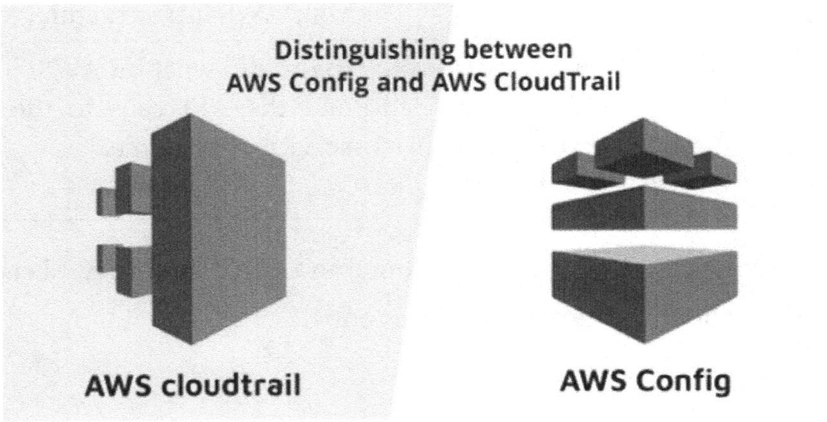

Figure 108

Difference between Cloud Watch and Cloud Trail:

No.	CloudWatch	CloudTrail
1	CloudWatch focuses on the activity of AWS services and resources, reporting on their health and performance.	CloudTrail is a log of all actions that have taken place inside your environment.
2	AWS CloudWatch is a monitoring service for AWS cloud resources and the applications you run on AWS.	AWS CloudTrail is a service that enables governance, compliance, operational, and risk auditing of your AWS account. Moreover, with CloudTrail, you can log, continuously monitor, and retain account activity related to actions across your AWS infrastructure.
3	What is happening on AWS?" and logging all the events for a particular service or application.	"Who did what on AWS?" and the API calls to the service or resource.

Lets study it more, login to account and get hands dirty. Lets move to last but one chapter of this book.

♦ ♦

Day 9
Lab 1

CHAPTER *Nine*

Database in Cloud

CHAPTER POINTS

- **What kind of database available in the cloud?**
- **Does it have a No-SQL database?**
- **Does the cloud have a traditional Relational database (RDBMS)?**
- **Do we have to prepare a server for hosting a database?**

9.1 Introduction to Database in Cloud

AWS offers a wide range of entirely accomplished, purpose-built, and mutually relational and non-relational database facilities. This is specially planned to handle any thoughtful of application requests such as entirely accomplished database facilities, a data warehouse for analytics, an in-memory data stock for storing, and so on, AWS has got it all.

You will discover an AWS Database Service for objective about any type of database necessities. One can import a prevailing MySQL, Oracle, or Microsoft SQL database hooked on Amazon's databases or even built their own relational or NoSQL databases from scratch.

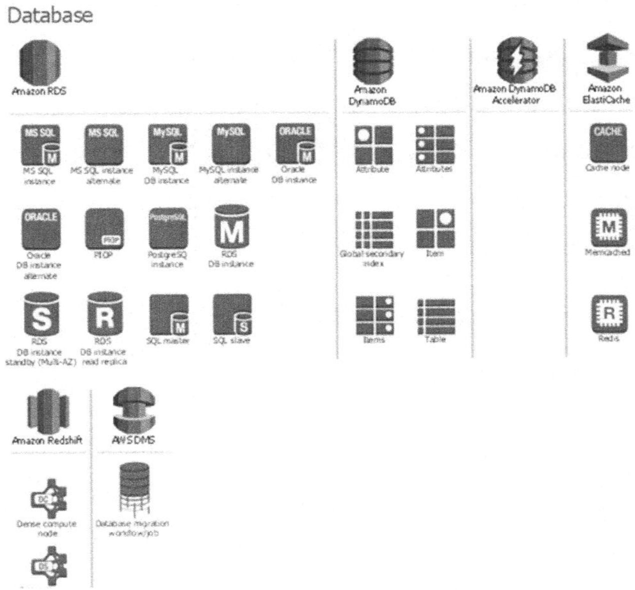

Figure 109

Relation Database System (RDS): In RDS, data is stored in tabular format, where it has rows and columns to store the data. It uses Standard Query Language (SQL) for any Data Manipulation Action (DML). Such as insert, update, and delete it is performed using SQL. AWS has the following RDS database service.

- Amazon RDS
- Amazon Redshift
- Amazon Aurora

Key-value Database: The key-value database is a type of NoSQL database. It can be used when the process of having a value attached to a key is used to store data. It means that the data is formed of two elements, keys and values.

- Amazon DynamoDB

In-Memory Database: This type of database is principally built on the main memory for server data storage. Fundamentally, an in-memory database retains the entire data in the RAM. It means that each time you access the data, you can only contact the main memory and not any disk. The purpose that the main memory is quicker than any disk is the reason why in-memory databases are so common.

- Amazon ElastiCache

9.2 RDS Database

A database manager can create, configure, manage, and delete an Amazon RDS instance, which is cloud database environs, alongside the compute and storage resources it uses. Provisional on which database engine an admin chooses, they can spin up several databases or schemas.

Amazon RDS confines each user to a total of 40 database instances per account. AWS enforces advance limitations for Oracle and SQL server instances, a user can only have up to 10 of each.

RDS database engines: An AWS user can create up to six different types of database engines within Amazon RDS.

1. **RDS for MySQL:** RDS is well-suited with the MySQL open-source relational database management system.
2. **RDS for PostgreSQL:** RDS is cordial with the PostgreSQL open source object-relational database management system.
3. **RDS for MariaDB:** RDS is well-matched with MariaDB, a community-developed offshoot of MySQL.
4. **RDS for SQL Server:** RDS is well-suited with Microsoft SQL Server, a relational database management system.
5. **RDS for Oracle Database:** RDS is cordial with several editions of Oracle Database which includes both multiple bring-your-own-license and license-included versions.

Figure 110

6. **Amazon Aurora:** It is compatible with MySQL and PostgreSQL, a registered AWS relational database engine.

Amazon RDS adds provision for major and minor versions of database engines concluded time, and an admin can state an engine version when they build a database instance. In maximum cases, Amazon RDS can upkeep developer code, applications, and tools that are already in use with existing databases.

Amazon Redshift: It is a fast and entirely managed data warehouse facility in the cloud. Amazon upholds that the Redshift data warehouse conveys ten times quicker performance than other data warehouses consuming Machine Learning practices. The Redshift data warehouse can be topped up to petabytes or more as per the requirements.

9.3 Key-value Database

DynamoDB: Amazon DynamoDB is a fast, entirely managed, and flexible NoSQL database. It also provisions document-based data. AWS upholds that DynamoDB distributes single-digit millisecond performance at any scale. DynamoDB emanates with built-in Security, Backup, and Restore features.

Subsequently, DynamoDB is a NoSQL database, it does not entail any schema. In DynamoDB, there are three principal components:

1. Tables: In DynamoDB, the pool of data is called a table. It is not a structured table with a fixed number of rows and columns.
2. Items: Tables in DynamoDB contain one or more items.

Items are made up of a group of uniquely identifiable attributes.

3. Attributes: Attributes are the data elements or values that reside in each item. They are equivalent to data values in a relational database that resides in a particular cell of a table.

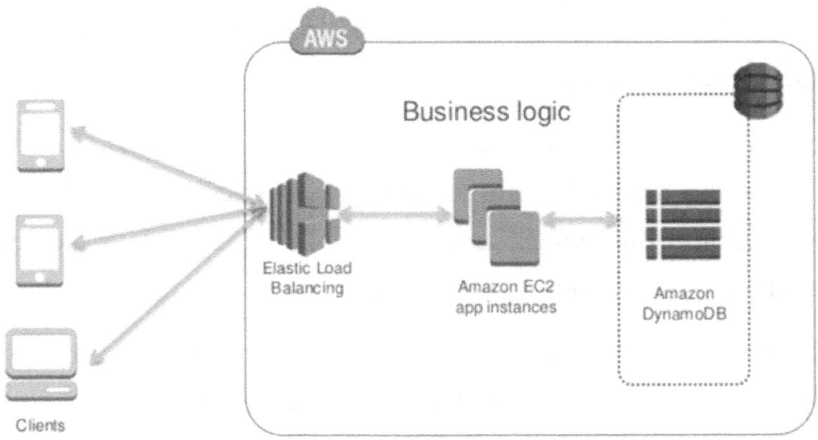

Figure 111

The difference between DynamoDB and RDS are as follows:

No.	DynamoDB	RDS
1	It is a No-SQL database.	These are the SQL/ Relational database.
2	Simple data model and transactions.	Relational data model and transactions.
3	It has a range of queries and simple updates.	It has a complex kind of join and updates.
4	Database scaling depends on application and DBA-architect.	Seamless, on-demand scaling based on application demand.

9.4 In-memory Database

An in-memory database is a type of purpose-built database that relies primarily on memory for data storage, in contrast to databases that store data on disk or SSDs. In-memory databases are designed to attain minimal response time by eliminating the need to access disks. Because all data is stored and managed exclusively in the main memory, it is at risk of being lost upon a process or server failure. In-memory databases can persist data on disks by storing each operation in a log or by taking snapshots.

Elastic Cache: Amazon ElastiCache is a fully accomplished caching service that bids high-performance, cost-effective, and scalable caching solutions. Amazon ElastiCache offers two caching engines, namely, Memcached and Redis.

Amazon Elasti Cache is a Caching-as-a-Service from Amazon Web Services. AWS streamlines setting up, managing, and scaling a circulated in-memory cache setting in the cloud. It offers a high-performance, scalable, and cost-effective caching resolution. AWS eradicates the difficulty allied with arranging and managing a distributed cache environment. The Amazon ElastiCache documentation helps us to acquire that ElastiCache has structures to progress consistency for critical production deployments, including:

- Automatic detection and recovery from cache node disasters.
- Automatic failover (Multi-AZ) of a failed primary cluster to a read replica in Redis replication groups.
- Flexible Availability Zone placement of nodes and clusters.

- Incorporation with other Amazon Web Services such as Amazon EC2, CloudWatch, CloudTrail, and Amazon SNS, to provide a safe, high-performance, accomplished in-memory caching solution.

Amazon ElastiCache offers two caching engines, Memcached and Redis. You can easily transfer your current Memcached or Redis caching implementation to Amazon ElastiCache. In your application, only change the Memcached/Redis endpoints.

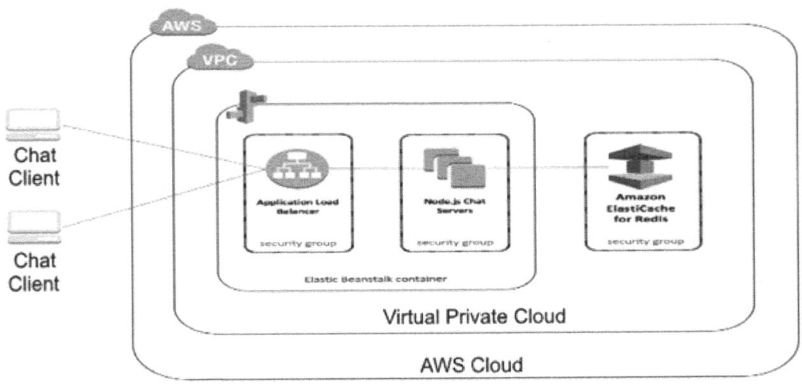

Figure 112

It is introductory knowledge of database in cloud. Lets move to costing part of cloud.

♦ ♦

Day 10

CHAPTER
Ten

Cost Calculator

CHAPTER POINTS

- **How will costing be charged?**
- **Before working on any resource, can we do a calculation for it?**
- **What are do's and don't in the cloud?**

10.1 Introduction to Cost Calculator

Let us see the financial part of cloud computing. How your bill is being calculated? What are dos and don'ts?

AWS has TCO, which is the Total Cost of Ownership calculator.

AWS Total Cost of Ownership (TCO) Calculator is used to match the cost of running systems in an in-premises or colocation environment to AWS. Describe the in-premises or colocation configuration to produce a detailed cost comparison with AWS. You can switch between the basic and advanced views to provide additional configuration details.

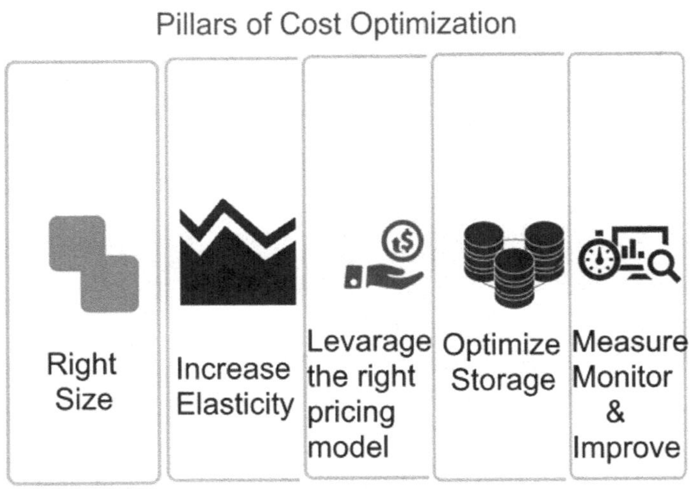

Figure 113

AWS Simple Monthly Calculator: Amazon Elastic Compute Cloud (Amazon EC2) is a web service that provides resizable compute capacity in the cloud. It is designed to make web-scale computing easier for developers. Amazon Elastic Block Store (EBS) provides persistent storage to Amazon EC2 instances.

Amazon EC2 Pricing: Pay only for what you use. There is no minimum fee. Estimate your monthly bill using the AWS Simple Monthly Calculator. The prices listed are based on the region in which your instance is running. For a detailed comparison between On-Demand Instances, Reserved Instances, and Spot Instances, see Amazon EC2 Instance Purchasing Options.

Amazon S3 Calculator: Amazon Web Services team has created a cost calculator that lets you plan costing that is liable on your part.

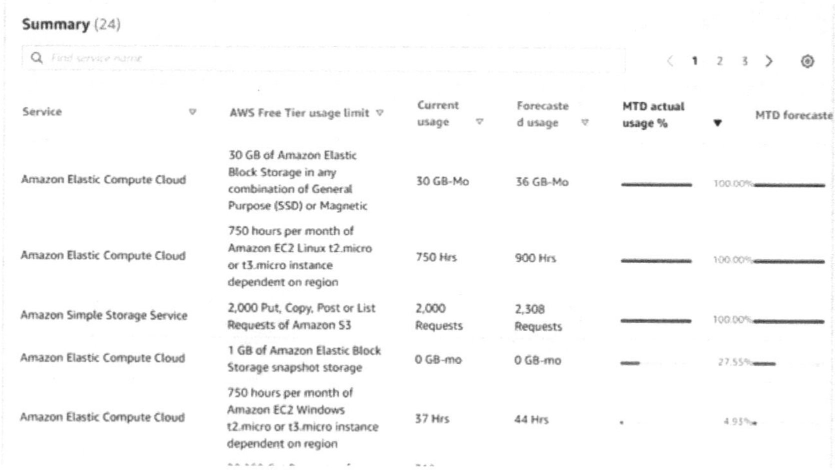

Summary (24)

Service	AWS Free Tier usage limit	Current usage	Forecasted usage	MTD actual usage %	MTD forecaste
Amazon Elastic Compute Cloud	30 GB of Amazon Elastic Block Storage in any combination of General Purpose (SSD) or Magnetic	30 GB-Mo	36 GB-Mo		100.00%
Amazon Elastic Compute Cloud	750 hours per month of Amazon EC2 Linux t2.micro or t3.micro instance dependent on region	750 Hrs	900 Hrs		100.00%
Amazon Simple Storage Service	2,000 Put, Copy, Post or List Requests of Amazon S3	2,000 Requests	2,308 Requests		100.00%
Amazon Elastic Compute Cloud	1 GB of Amazon Elastic Block Storage snapshot storage	0 GB-mo	0 GB-mo		27.55%
Amazon Elastic Compute Cloud	750 hours per month of Amazon EC2 Windows t2.micro or t3.micro instance dependent on region	37 Hrs	44 Hrs		4.93%

AWS Free Tier: The AWS Free Tier is planned to enable you to get hands-on practice with AWS Cloud Services at no charge for 12 months after you sign up.

Since it is limited access to every component, you can check, how much you have utilized. Login to your account, go to Billing, on the dashboard, you will see "Top Free Tier Services by Usage."

Click on "View All" button, and you will get detailed information on all resources.

AWS Total Cost of Ownership (TCO) Calculator: Figure shows the calculator. You can use this calculator to compare the cost of running your applications in an in-premises or colocation environment to AWS. Also, describe your in-premises or colocation configuration to produce a detailed cost comparison with AWS. Moreover, you can switch between the basic and advanced views to provide additional configuration details.

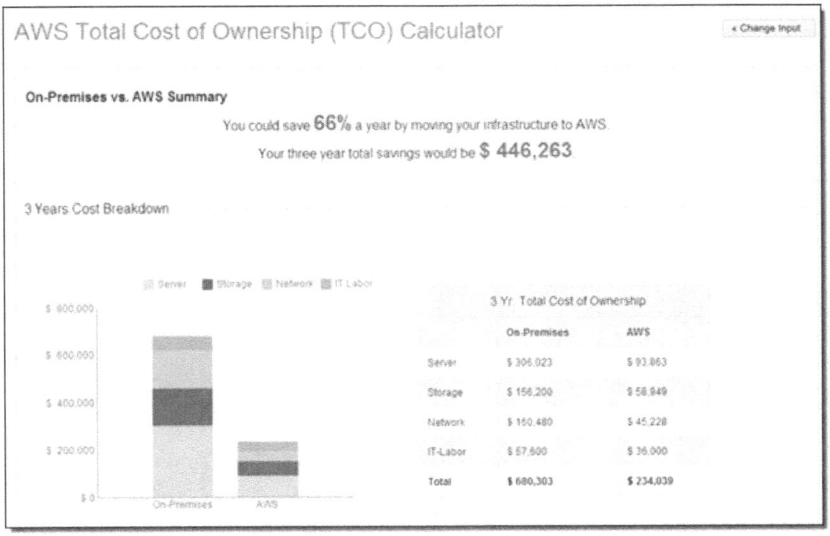

Figure 114

Using all these tools, you can forecast the cost of resources you are utilizing for your account. With this, we have come to the end of this book. Hope you liked it? We will see detailed information on each tool in other books.

You have done this in 10 days. Now you have basic cloud computing knowledge. Lets meet in next book for detail explanations of these topics.